I0621220

California

South Coast

Wineries Guide

By

Corey Lee Wilson

California South Coast Wineries Guide

All rights reserved. No part of this book may be reproduced in any manner without the express written consent of the publisher, except in the case of brief excerpts in all types of written media. All inquiries for such can be made below.

All of our **California Winery Guides** are published in partnership with Fratire Publishing LLC and can be purchased in bulk with special discounts for schools, libraries and associations. All inquiries for such can be made below to Fratire Publishing LLC.

FRATIRE PUBLISHING LLC
4533 Temescal Canyon Rd. # 308
Corona CA 92883-4659
www.FratirePublishing.com
FratirePublishing@att.net
1 + (951) 638-5502

FratirePublishing
Relevant Books for **SAPIENT** Beings

Copyright © Sep. 2023 1st edition, Sep. 2025 2nd edition.

LCCN 2023914463

Pdf and Epub versions can be purchased directly at Fratire Publishing LLC, California, USA at https://www.fratirepublishing.com/winery-guides.

- WINE-SC-25-PDF (pdf)
- WINE-SC-25-EPUB (epub)

Paperbacks printed and eBooks distributed domestically and internationally are by Ingram Spark in La Vergne, Tennessee, USA and both versions can be purchased at Amazon.

- ISBN 978-1-953319-49-4 (Paperback)
- ISBN 978-1-953319-38-8 (eBook)

Special thanks for the winery maps by W. Clark Simpson at w.clark.simpson@gmail.com, cover design by Jenny Barroso at j20graphics@gmail.com, American Viticultural Areas (AVA) data from the California Department of Alcoholic Beverage Control (ABC), and wineries licensing data from the USA Alcohol and Tobacco Tax and Trade Bureau (TTB).

For more information about **California Winery Guides** visit our website at www.californiawineryguides.com and learn more about California's nine spectacular wine regions and interesting facts and statistics about them.

Cover Credit: Renzoni Winery in California's Temecula Valley at sunset. Photo courtesy of Matthew Burlile.

Contents

An Introduction to California Wineries

California is the largest and most important wine region in the USA. It accounts for the southern two-thirds of the country's west coast and spans almost ten degrees of latitude. With mountains, valleys, plains and plateaus, California's topography is as complex as its climate, offering winegrowers an abundant number of terroir (soils) from which to grow grapes and produce a diverse variety of wines.

Today, California hosts some of the world's largest wine companies and is also home to hundreds of boutique wineries, some of which attract astronomical prices for their vintages. Whether through mass production or single-vineyard artisanal winemaking, California produces 90 percent of American-made wine, supplies more than 60 percent of all wine consumed in the country, and is home to 43% of American wineries.

The state's viticultural history dates back more than 200 years from the Spanish missions. However, ever since the 1976 Judgment of Paris, in which a Cabernet Sauvignon from Stags' Leap Winery and a Chardonnay from Chateau Montelena defeated wines from Bordeaux and Burgundy, there has been much debate in the wine industry about the unique California style.

Most critics agree it all starts with very fruit-forward wines that make extensive use of the optimal growing conditions throughout California's vast geography and unique climate zones to pick very ripe fruit. These optimal growing conditions throughout California's nine wine regions, covering more than 4,700 wineries (but only half are licensed for tasting), lead to wines that are very lush and rich in flavor, with a wide variety (varietals) to choose from.

Arguably one of the top winery destinations and wine tasting locations in the world, California's cornucopia of wineries, distinctive wine regions, and extensive number of varietals—are hard to beat, and the state is ranked fourth in the world if you count the number of wineries that dot America's largest Pacific Coast state.

About California Winery Guides

At **California Winery Guides** our goal is to publish the most complete and up-to-date California winery guides so that everyone—from novice to connoisseur, can enjoy the bounty and diversity of California's wine harvest and the savory juices and varietals that come with them—year after year.

Along with this annual goal as our motivation comes our mission to make the vast array and assortment of California grapes, wines and wineries more visible and accessible—and in the process, enhance and expand wine appreciation, wine tasting, and wine tourism throughout California's nine wine regions.

Because there is so much to see, smell, taste, and savor throughout California's wine regions—we have created nine winery guides to compliment the nine distinct wine regions listed below.

Our easy to use winery guides have no equal—and we believe you're the best wine critic. We provide the most essential and up-to-date information for each winery so you can make your own decisions.

At the center of our winery guides are the A to Z wineries listings, including each winery's name, address, email address (if they have one), online link—plus their wine tasting hours, amenities, varietals, and a brief winery introduction.

As to which wineries we list? We list all of them, by county and have no preference or bias as to their size, reputation, awards won, how long they've been established, etc.

The geographical focus of this particular California wineries guidebook is the South Coast wine region of California. Plus, we cover all of California's other 8 wine growing regions (listed below) with their own wineries guidebook, like this one. Enjoy!

The nine wine regions of California from north to south:

- Sierra Foothills & Central Valley
- North Coast
- Sonoma
- Napa
- Bay Area
- Monterey
- San Luis Obispo
- Santa Barbara
- South Coast

How Our Wineries Guide Works

Our easy to use and comprehensive winery guide for the 21st century that has no equal. We believe you're the best critic, so we provide you with the most essential and up-to-date information for each winery so you can make your own decisions. As to which wineries we list? We list all of them, provided they have "posted" and "defined" tasting schedules and meet the criteria below. Furthermore, we have no preference as to their size, reputations, awards won, how long they've been established, etc. We're not pretentious.

At the heart of each winery guidebook, in the central section, are the A to Z listings of every winery located in that guidebook's wine regions or counties.

The information covered for each winery is clearly and simply laid out that includes their name, address, phone number, email address (if they have one), online address, days and hours open, amenities, varietals, and a brief introduction about the winery.

The only exceptions for excluding a bonded winery will be if their ABC Class 2– Winegrower license and/or other local licenses are not active, they haven't opened their doors yet, don't offer tasting in any type of venue, don't have a website, or Facebook page, or listing in any of the popular winery review/travel sites, or some informational online source like Yelp that we can include the link of, so our readers can follow it and learn more about that particular winery.

Regarding days and hours open, we specify their wine tasting hours of operation, days of the week for tasting, and if reservations are required ahead of visiting the winery for tasting. Even if no reservations are required, it's always smart to contact the winery ahead of time, particularly the boutique wineries, at least 72 hours in advance, if you're not already in the immediate area so as not to waste a trip and be disappointed if they're not open. It happens!

Following, are a winery's typical amenities such as providing comedy, private or public events, food (can range from breads, cheeses, crackers, cold cuts, sandwiches, pizzas, food trucks, catered food, to complete dinners), lodging, music, picnic area, tasting (which can be limited to only off-site tasting events or local pick-up only), winery and/or cellar tours, weddings, and a wine club if they have one. WE also note it the winery is an urban winery/wine bar instead.

Then we list in alphabetical order their varietals but because most wineries have their own unique brand of blends, we don't list them in order to keep this section manageable. With that noted, most wineries will have a few to a wide assortment of blends, so check them out by all means because this is where wineries can be creative and unique and stand out from the rest. The same goes for roses, sparkling wines, and late harvest / desert wines.

Lastly, there is a brief introduction about the winery in their own words—not ours.

If you're a novice tasting wines at a tasting room for the first time, we made it easy for you to find them. If you're a wine connoisseur with an extensive knowledge and appreciation of wine, the digital versions of this winery guide can help you filter the types of wine varietals you're looking for.

There you have it, a fast, easy, organized, and updated wineries tasting guidebook at your fingertips so you can spend more time planning your wine tasting, identifying and selecting the wineries that suit your wine palette, and getting the most pleasure and satisfaction out of it when you're out and about wine tasting.

So with all this great winery info at hand, what are you waiting for? Go wine tasting and be sure to mention to your friends, family, and organization—you read about their winery in our wineries guide.

The Nine Wine Regions of California

This California wineries guidebook is part of a series of guidebooks covering the nine wine growing regions in California. In many wine enthusiast circles, there's a consensus on the boundaries of some of the wine region—but for others, there is no unifying consensus.

Nonetheless, at **California Winery Guides** we based our regional designations on a number of factors using geographic location, overall size, distinct wine appellations, wine growing associations, and other considerations explained in more detail below.

We also factored in the sheer number of wineries (4,500 plus and more on the way every year), their concentration throughout the state of California, proximity of wineries to major populations centers (like the Bay Area and Los Angeles for example), distance and drive times to get to each wine region, and the wine region's climate, topography, and geology.

In addition to the above, where a previously defined wine region covered a large area and/or many wineries in a particular area, and to align each wine region more closely to their respective travel, convention, and tourist bureau definitions that help define their regional boundaries, we separated the wine regions into smaller and more distinct areas—thus the nine wine regions.

A perfect example of this regarding the geographic size of a wine region separated into smaller areas is the California Central Coast. The Central Coast covers twelve California counties (that include eight Bay Area, two in the Monterey area, and two more in the redefined Central Coast area of Santa Barbara and San Luis Obispo counties), a combined area larger than many of America's smaller states.

Almost as long as Florida's 360-mile-long eastern coastline, the Central Coast wine region covers a significant area from the NW corner of Marin County, all the way down to the SW corner of Santa Barbara County, a distance of 350 miles and close to six hours of drive time from one end to the other along US Highway 101.

For these reasons, the Central Coast wine region is divided into four smaller and more cohesive regions, with the Bay Area (eight counties and over 300 wineries) taking up the north end, the Monterey area (two counties approaching 100 wineries) holding the middle, and the revised and resized Central Coast region consisting of San Luis Obispo and Santa Barbara counties area (two counties and over 400 wineries), taking up the south end.

The North Coast wine region is another example of splitting up a large number and high concentration (1,000 plus) of wineries. These wineries are concentrated into the previously designated and all-encompassing North Coast wine region covering Napa and Sonoma counties, along with the four counties northward consisting of Mendocino, Humboldt, Lake, and Trinity counties (containing more than 100 wineries combined).

The Napa and Sonoma counties and wine regions, to no one's surprise, have always held their own distinct wine regions of California with close to 1,000 wineries combined.

Lastly, in defining which counties to include in the Bay Area wine region, we included all the counties bordering the Bay Area's coastlines (except Sonoma and Napa counties). To be precise, if you zoom in on a map of the Bay Area, Napa County doesn't touch the bay, but almost does.

So how many bays, in the Bay Area system, are there besides the San Francisco Bay that these eight Bay Area counties touch? If we head north of San Fracisco Bay into San Pablo Bay and then head east towards Sacramento, we come to Suisun Bay, and the lesser known Grizzly and Honkers bays adjoining Suisun Bay.

However, included in the Bay Area region is one county that doesn't touch any of the bays, and it's Santa Cruz County, an outlier. True, it touches Monterey Bay, but it's history, economy, and inter-county relationships are more strongly developed and aligned with the Bay Area counties of San Mateo and Santa Clara to the north than Monterey County to the south.

Finally, the Sierra Foothills and Central Valley wine regions (with over 300 wineries) are combined because their winery locations, although covering a very large area but sparsely populated with wineries compared to Napa and Sonoma counties) follow a relatively narrow band of California real estate in a north-west to south-east trajectory within the two ends of the Central Valley (Sacramento Valley to the north and San Joaquin Valley to the south).

Along this trajectory, to the east of the Central Valley, sits the Sierra Nevada foothills and their wineries, aptly named the Sierra Foothills winery region.

Below the foothills are the major cities of Sacramento, Modesto, Fresno, and Bakersfield and where we find the Central Valley wineries.

Altogether, these 9 wine regions are listed below from north to south below including their respective counties or county, as follows:

- Sierra Foothills & Central Valley (Amador, Butte, Calaveras, El Dorado, Fresno, Kern, Lassen, Madera, Mariposa, Modoc, Nevada, Placer, Sacramento, San Joaquin, Shasta, Siskiyou, Stanislaus, Tehama, Tulare, Tuolumne, Yolo & Yuba counties)

- North Coast (Humboldt, Lake, Mendocino & Trinity counties)

- Sonoma (Sonoma County)

- Napa (Napa County)

- Bay Area (Alameda, Contra Costa, Marin, Santa Clara, Santa Cruz, San Francisco, San Mateo & Solano counties)

- Monterey (Monterey & San Benito counties)

- San Luis Obispo County

- Santa Barbara County

- South Coast (Los Angeles, Orange, Riverside, San Bernardino, San Diego & Ventura counties)

Please note the year used in our guidebook for when a winery was established, is the earliest one recorded and listed on the Alcoholic Beverage Control (ABC) licensing website page, that lists the date a winery's Class 2 Winegrower license was first issued (activated).

To learn more about when the other California wine region guidebooks are available, please check out the Winery Guides section of the Fratire Publishing website at https://www.fratirepublishing.com/california-winery-guides.

Wineries Guidebook Promotion and Updates

Please note for every winery who actively promotes our winery guides to their guests, membership, subscribers, etc.—will receive a free epub version every year for as long as they continue do this. All that's required is to proudly display your region's wineries guidebook in a visible location in your tasting room as pictured above.

To claim your free yearly epub version of our wineries guidebook, please contact us by email using the subject title Free Wineries Guide at fratirepublishing@att.net along with your winery name, contact person, mailing address, phone number, email address and website or social media link and we'll mail you this promotional display package with paperback guidebook free of charge.

When you receive your free shipment, simply remove both rubber bands and place the guidebook in the upright book holder, then place the TAKE ONE CARD business card holder in front of the bookstand, and position both in a highly visible location in your tasting room.

If you run out of cards, or the guidebook becomes soiled, or the two holders are damaged, or the guidebook is missing—no problem—simply let us know and we'll replace them for free.

Lastly, is your winery missing from this guidebook? if so and you're a licensed winery with tasting hours, please contact us by email using the subject title Winery Update at fratirepublishing@att.net with the desired/corrected info so we can add/or correct your winery listing in the next edition. The same goes for updating info for existing wineries when changes occur to their hours, amenities, varietals and any other vital data.

California Wine History & Industry

The California wine industry literally put down its roots in 1769, when Padre Junipero Serra began his chain of missions in San Diego by planting grape seeds and vines. Eventually it stretched to Sonoma, more than 650 miles to the north.

The California wine industry owes its success to many fathers. One was a key vigneron, Jean-Louis Vignes, who established vineyards near what is now Los Angeles in 1834 and began the commercial wine industry.

The California wine industry began to really take shape in the early 1900s. By the mid-19th century, California was producing millions of gallons of wine per year and was the largest wine producer in the United States until two disasters struck.

The first was an infestation of phylloxera, the louse that attacks vine roots, which by 1915 destroyed 250,000 acres of California vineyards. Then, in 1919, Prohibition was enacted, outlawing the manufacture, transportation, sale, and possession of alcoholic beverages. Hundreds of California wineries were forced to close. By the time Prohibition was repealed in 1933, most wineries were in sad shape, having been neglected for years.

The University of California played a major role in moving the rekindled industry to quality, defining climate zones for growing fine wine grapes and establishing strict sanitation and quality production standards for the state's wineries.

In the 1960s, the California wine industry began to lay the foundation for a surge in wine sales and the industry received a boost in 1976 when a Franco-Californian blind tasting was held in Paris to commemorate the U.S. Bicentennial.

To the surprise of everyone—especially the French—two upstart wineries from the Napa Valley finished in first place. The tasting, known as "The Judgment of Paris," triggered an avalanche of global publicity for California wine, even prompting some French winemakers to join forces with or buy California properties.

Several other trends soon emerged to shape the market further. The move toward cooler climates proved as important as the recognition that controlling crop yields, using natural winemaking techniques, and fermenting wines in toasty oak barrels would lead to finer, more complex wines.

The spread of skilled California winemakers, with their varied tastes and inspirations, meant that a broad spectrum of wine styles—from elegant and finely structured to powerful and fruit-filled—would be made right there in the state.

The Modern Wine Industry

There are now more than 100 grape varieties grown in California, including a mix of the most popular French, Italian and Spanish grapes. Moreover, California wineries now produce all types of wine, including sparkling, dessert and fortified wines.

The primary focus, however, is on the "noble" grape varieties, including Cabernet Sauvignon, Merlot, Syrah, Pinot Noir, Chardonnay, Sauvignon Blanc and Riesling. In addition, other popular grape varieties include Zinfandel, Petite Sirah, Grenache, Mourvèdre, Malbec, Cabernet Franc, Roussanne, Nebbiolo and Sangiovese.

On a statewide basis, Cabernet Sauvignon and Chardonnay are the two most important grape varieties. Out of the total 525,000 acres planted in California, nearly 95,000 are dedicated to Chardonnay and 80,000 are dedicated to Cabernet Sauvignon. Interestingly, nearly one-quarter (25%) of all vineyards in the Golden State are dedicated to organic, biodynamic, and sustainable winemaking practices.

Today, California hosts some of the world's largest wine companies and its winegrowing regions span the entire state and reflect a diverse and distinctive mix of winegrape varieties in significantly different locations, or appellations. It is also home to a wide array of boutique wineries, some of which attract astronomical prices for their cult wines. Furthermore, California is the fourth leading wine producer in the world!

Whether through mass production or single-vineyard artisanal winemaking, California produces 90 percent of American-made wine. It also supplies more than 60 percent of all wine consumed in the country (with the rest shipped internationally). A record 211.9 million cases were produced in 2011.

American Viticultural Areas (AVAs) in California

In the United States, the legal term for a wine appellation is an American Viticultural Area, or AVA, and corresponds to a unique geographical grape-growing area that has officially been given appellation status by the Bureau of Alcohol, Tobacco and Firearms (ABC).

Across the Golden State, thousands of acres of new vineyards were planted, and by 1980 the Bureau of Alcohol, Tobacco and Firearms approved and published labeling standards, allowing California to establish viticultural areas based on historical, climatic and geographic characteristics and to feature these areas on wine labels.

Each American Viticulture Area has a distinct "persona" that divides it from the other AVAs. The distinct persona is mainly categorized by climate, geology and elevation. No surprise, Napa Valley is the original California AVA. For a California wine label to display an appellation name, 85% of the fruit in the wine must come from that appellation.

There are 154 American Viticultural Areas (AVAs) in California, a number which is ever increasing. From Mendocino County in the North Coast all the way down to the southern border with Mexico, from coastal regions lining the Pacific Ocean to vineyards flanking the Sierra Nevada foothills, each of the areas boast characteristics that are uniquely their own. These local differences support the cultivation of a wide range of grape varieties and shape a diverse range of wines.

California Wine Regions & Tourism

California Wine Regions

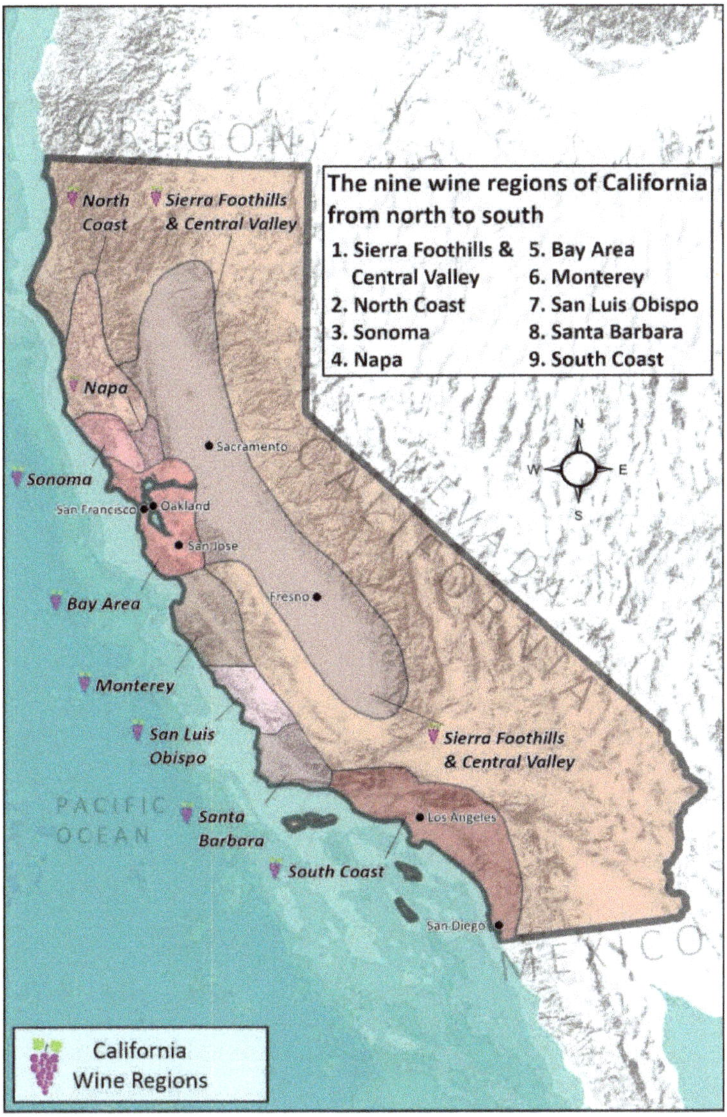
OREGON
North Coast
Sierra Foothills & Central Valley
The nine wine regions of California from north to south
1. Sierra Foothills & Central Valley
2. North Coast
3. Sonoma
4. Napa
5. Bay Area
6. Monterey
7. San Luis Obispo
8. Santa Barbara
9. South Coast
Napa
Sacramento
Sonoma
San Francisco
Oakland
San Jose
N
W
E
S
CALIFORNIA
NEVADA
Bay Area
Fresno
Monterey
San Luis Obispo
Sierra Foothills & Central Valley
PACIFIC OCEAN
Santa Barbara
Los Angeles
South Coast
San Diego
MEXICO
California Wine Regions

California wine country is a big draw for luxury travelers, according to a new report from the Wine Institute. Between its stunning fruit-filled vineyards and wealth of standout sips, it's no secret why California is such a popular destination for wine lovers.

California's wine industry continues to grow, with the number of bonded wineries having increased from 3200+ in 2011 to 4200+ in 2020. To be exact, in 2022, there were 4,876 bonded wineries in California representing 43% of the total number of wineries in the USA.

According to an online survey of more than 2,000 U.S. adults who had recently visited California wine country, nearly 50 percent stayed in luxury hotels (48.3% four-star, 25.6% five-star) versus a national norm of about 15 percent staying in the equivalent of five-star properties.

Visitors use a variety of resources in deciding which regions and wineries to visit and most often rely on word-of-mouth recommendations (62.3%) and general Internet searches (43.9%). While most California wine region trips are driven by leisure vacations (32.6%) or weekend getaways (26.2%), nearly one in ten trips (8.5%) is an add-on to a business or convention trip.

The Wine Institute commissioned the study with support from a USDA grant. It was conducted by Destination Analysts of San Francisco and was fielded in late 2016. In the study, a California wine tourist was defined as someone who had visited a California wine region for leisure within the past three years to capture both high-involvement and casual wine tourists.

Highlights

The profile of the California wine country visitor is consistent with wine drinker demographics. The average age of visitors to California wine country is 43.9 years old, with Baby Boomers accounting for 39.5 percent, Gen Xers 21.9 percent and Millennials 36.1 percent.

The majority of visitors are married (68.3%), resides in an urban (45.6%) or suburban (44%) area and are slightly more likely to be female (53.7% vs. 46.3%). California wine region visitors are well-educated and have higher incomes compared to the national average leisure traveler.

More than 70 percent of California wine country visitors surveyed drink wine at least once a week with 36 percent drinking wine several times a week and nearly 20 percent imbibing daily. Nearly 60 percent consider wine "important" or "very important" to their lifestyles and see themselves as "very knowledgeable" about the beverage.

About 30 percent have been a member of one or more wine clubs in the past three years, suggesting the potential for growth in wine club sign-ups but also serving as a reminder that while many wine tourists may not join clubs they do purchase wine from other outlets and recommend them to others based on winery visits.

The vast majority of California wine visitors were highly satisfied with their trips and extremely likely to recommend the regions they visited to others. Over 70 percent of surveyed travelers preferred the California wine region they visited to out-of-state wine regions. About 73 percent found that the California wine region visited provided a "better" or "much better" experience.

Residents from outside of the state gave the California wine experience higher ratings than those from California. Nearly 79 percent of travelers from other states gave a top score (8 or above on a 10-point scale), compared to 72 percent of Californians. Finally, visits to a wine region greatly increased the likelihood of purchasing wines from that region when travelers returned home, especially among out-of-state visitors (64% very likely to purchase).

Word of mouth was by far the leading source of information (62%) for deciding what regions to visit, followed by general online search (44%), suggesting that social media and search optimization are very important communications channels for wineries and wine regions. Interestingly, wine magazines edged out travel magazines as an information source, while printed wine region maps came out higher than both (not everything has gone digital).

The survey asked visitors to respond to a series of questions on regions they had visited in the past three years. Based on an analysis of responses, visitors to less well-known or remote wine regions of the state most closely mirror the high-involvement wine drinker versus visitors to more well-known regions.

A higher percentage of visitors to lesser known regions regard wine as important to their lifestyles, are members of wine clubs and consider themselves knowledgeable about wine. This likely reflects both the dedication of high-involvement wine country visitors to seeking out new regions and a larger number of casual visitors to well-known regions—areas of opportunity for both wineries and regions.

Climate & Soil

Have you ever wondered how this sun-kissed state is able to produce such a wide array of high-quality wines? The terroir and geography differ considerably throughout the state, ranging from warm inland valleys to cooler coastal areas.

California winegrowing conditions are governed by proximity to the Pacific Ocean. Cold ocean air turns to fog as it moves up the valleys to cool the land. The cycle of hot days followed by cool, foggy nights lengthens the ripening period and increases the flavor intensity of grapes.

Almost all of the fine wine regions of California are located in areas influenced at least somewhat by the Pacific fog bank. Further inland, consistently hot, sunny areas are used more for fruit and vegetable farming and bulk wine production.

Soils and climates vary substantially throughout California. A complex combination of variables are in play. These include altitude, latitude and proximity to the cool waters of the Pacific Ocean.

In summer, the cold inshore waters of the Pacific help to create a fog bank just off the coast. As the inland air warms and rises, cold fog is sucked in to fill the space. In extreme cases, fog has been known to travel as far as 100 miles (160km) inland, cooling and refreshing the land as it goes. However, mountainous terrain between a vineyard and the Pacific limits the influence of a maritime climate. This relationship can vary widely across the state creating a wide variety of microclimates.

Generally, the cooler regions closer to the coast are better suited to cool climate grape varieties such as Pinot Noir and Chardonnay. Further inland where the climate is much hotter, some of California's most famous red wine is made from Cabernet Sauvignon. Zinfandel produces some outstanding examples throughout the state.

Takeaways

While the premium wine business showed continued success in 2022, overall wine consumption showed a second year of negative growth. Future sales weigh on the industry's ability to appeal to a new generation of consumers.

Consumers younger than 60 have a lower share of wine consumption compared to what they did in 2007. Consumers older than 60 are the population bands where there is still growth.

While older consumers are paying more for premium wine, younger buyers are increasingly less engaged with the wine category because 35% of 21–29-year-old consumers drink alcohol, but not wine. That number drops 7 percentage points to 28% for individuals 50–59 years old. Of those consumers who left that group, two percentage points moved to being at least marginal wine consumers. Meanwhile, five percent are now abstaining from drinking alcohol.

South Coast Wineries A to Z

South Coast Winery Region AVAs

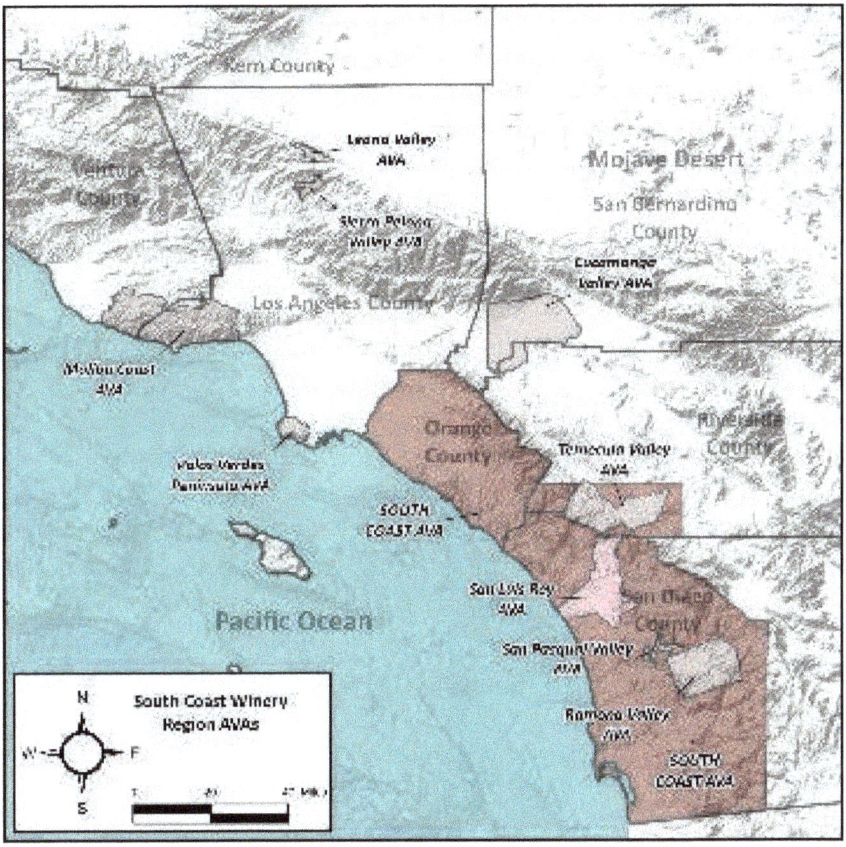

The South Coast wine region stretches from San Diego County and the border of Mexico on the south to Ventura County in the north. Today, every single county in Southern California has vineyards, wineries, and urban tasting rooms. Visitors to the South Coast region's 250 wineries that offer tasting along with urban tasting rooms (sometimes referred to as wine bars) should keep in mind that the wine grape varietals that grow in cooler areas on the coast are often quite different than those grown in warm inland valleys—so be sure to try wineries across the region.

Geography

The South Coast American Viticultural Area (AVA) includes grape-growing areas in six counties: San Diego, Riverside, Ventura, Los Angeles, San Bernardino, and Orange. While there are microclimates throughout these counties that depend on your exact elevation and distance from the ocean, generally the South Coast boasts warm weather cooled down by coastal breezes.

This is the perfect climate for Chardonnay, the grape of choice in Southern California. Zinfandel also thrives in the area, and some very old Zinfandel vines are still being used. You can also find high-quality Syrah and Cabernet Sauvignon produced in the region. Winemakers in the area are also experimenting with Rhone and Iberian grapes like other areas of California.

Weather

The South Coast wine region is further south than the wine regions in Europe, and in fact is closer in latitude to wine-producing regions in North Africa. While there are some vineyards in the warmer, inland valleys in the region, most vineyards in the South Coast are closer to the coast. The cooling influence of the Pacific Ocean helps to ensure that the grapes do not dry out.

While most vineyards in the region are to the west of the Sierra Pelona Mountains, closer to the Pacific Ocean, there are some notable exceptions. Vineyards in this hot, dry part of California need something to lower the temperature. While the breeze from the Pacific Ocean does this for most vineyards, some use high elevation to lower the temperature instead.

Soil (Terroir)

This region has incredible variety in soil types. If you're considering starting a vineyard in the South Coast, keep in mind that the exact soil type you're working with will inform which grape varietals will grow well. More mountainous areas in the region have either rocky shale soils or soils with a lot of granite. Areas at lower elevations have sandier soils. Consult a local expert about the types of grapes that will grow best at your location. Luckily, though, all of the soil types in the South Coast have excellent drainage, which is essential for vineyards.

6 Winery Areas (by County) of the South Coast Region

Most wine enthusiasts will be shocked to know the South Coast wine region has 250 wineries that offer tasting! Included in that number are urban wineries/wine bars (simply called "wineries" throughout this guidebook), and they tend to congregate around city centers and tourist hot spots.

With respect to Southern California geography that covers a large area and in consideration of the distances and travel time required in a day to visit these wineries, we've simply broken out the wineries by county and then listed them from A to Z. So how many wineries are there per the 6 counties? Here's a list below ranking counties with the largest number of wineries to the smallest number of wineries:

1. San Diego County: 117
2. Riverside County: 59
3. Ventura County: 31
4. Los Angeles County: 24
5. Orange County: 10
6. San Bernardino County: 9

For most intrepid wine tasters, a journey to the wineries located outside the cities that grow their own grapes in their vineyards, will take up most of your day, including commute time. For urban wineries/wine bars, that's not the case, and this is one of the advantages of tasting at these nearby locations.

Our advice is to pace yourself and limit the number of wineries for tasting to a bare minimum—no more than two or three. If you try to do more than that, your wine buzz will kick into high gear, and by the time, if not before you've finished your last tasting and hit the road again—your blood alcohol content could exceed the legal limit. Don't do that! Drink responsibly!

Furthermore, many of you will be pleased to know there are 13 AVAs in the South Coast region with each of them exhibiting unique geographical grape-growing soil, locations, and weather. That's a good thing because it gives wine seekers and tourists an ever growing and diverse portfolio of California wineries to tour, sample, and buy from depending on their tastes.

San Diego County Wine Region

San Diego County is the second most populous in California after Los Angeles County but it has the most number of wineries in the South Coast wine region. Most are concentrated around the Ramona area, east of Escondido, at higher elevations. Others, and their viticulture, takes place in the inland hills that run the length of the county. For the less adventurous, the San Diego has a strong urban winery presence.

With 100 plus wineries to choose from, and more on the way, San Diego has four AVAs within their county and they are the all-encompassing South Coast, Ramona Valley, San Pasqual Valley, and the resent San Luis Rey. The latter two can both be found in these hills, although there are many wineries scattered across the rest of San Diego County as part of the South Coast AVA that covers a much larger area.

Newly proposed AVAs in San Diego County include rancho Guejito of Escondido and Rancho Santa Fe approximately 25 miles north of San Diego next to the coast.

Viticulture has enjoyed a renaissance in San Diego County in the past 20 years and many new boutique producers are making excellent wine under the San Diego County AVA. Additionally, the regions also an important center of craft beer production.

The region is also popular with, and served by conveniently located urban tasting locations, with wine varietals procured from remote vineyards in the three local AVAs or other California wine regions, that are then produced locally on site.

History of Wine Production

The history of viticulture in San Diego County stretches right back to the time of the first Catholic missionaries in California. San Diego de Alcalá, established in 1769, was the first mission and the vineyard, that was planted then to make sacramental wine, is largely considered to be the first in California (although viticulture in nearby Mexico predates this by almost 200 years).

Commercial viniculture sprung up following the California Gold Rush of the 1850s, but Prohibition in the 1920s spelt the end of San Diego's wine industry until its resurrection in the 1990s.

Some of the wineries listed rose from the ashes of the 2007 Witch Creek and Guejito fires that burnt down many existing avocado groves that were later cleared and converted to planting grape varietals for new wineries taking their place.

Growing Conditions and Grape Varieties

San Diego County has a moderate Mediterranean climate, with hot, dry summers and mild winters. Despite this, most vineyards in the region are located close enough to the coast to benefit from cooling winds and fog from the Pacific Ocean. These temperature-moderating factors are enough to lengthen the growing season, ensuring grapes don't lose acidity as they ripen slowly.

Much of the county is covered by chaparral, a kind of low scrub that is similar to the garrigue of Languedoc-Roussillon in France and the fynbos of South Africa. This scrubland has sometimes been destructive to the vineyards of San Diego County so wildfires are not uncommon and in the past, vines have been destroyed.

The county is particularly noted for bold, ripe red wines made from Cabernet Sauvignon, Zinfandel and Petite Sirah. Vineyards of Chardonnay are found scattered throughout the cooler regions of the South Coast AVA.

Ramona Valley AVA

The Ramona Valley AVA is an American Viticultural Area in the larger San Diego County AVA in southern California. The region was awarded AVA status in 2006 because of its unique terroir, capable of producing rich, ripe examples of Cabernet Sauvignon, Petite Sirah, Tempranillo, Syrah, Barbera and Zinfandel.

Wineries here are generally tiny, boutique wineries; there are around three dozen in the local Vineyard Association plus over 60 independent vineyards. They produce a range of mostly red wines, with some whites made from Viognier, Marsanne and Roussanne, Sauvignon Blanc and Muscat Canelli (Muscat Blanc a Petits Grains).

The wider San Diego County was home to some of the first Vitis vinifera grapes in California, planted here in the late 1700s at the state's first Catholic mission. However, the modern winemaking industry in Ramona didn't really take off

25

until the 1990s, when pioneering vignerons began to explore the potential of the area.

Unfortunately, the dry climate of Ramona Valley means that bush fires are not uncommon, and the Cedar and Witch Creek fires of 2003 and 2007 respectively caused a lot of damage to the area.

The AVA covers an area surrounding the town of Ramona, 36 miles (58 kilometers) north-east of the city of San Diego. The town sits in a broad, bowl-shaped valley, and vineyards can be found on the surrounding hillsides at altitudes of up to 1400 feet (430 meters).

The climate in Ramona Valley is hot and dry, and its equidistance from the Pacific Ocean in the west and the Colorado Desert in the east means it feels climatic effects from both. The Pacific Ocean, 25 miles (40km) away, offers up morning fog and afternoon breezes, meaning that the temperatures at night are much lower than during the day.

This diurnal temperature shift is exacerbated by both the proximity of the desert and the altitude of the area. The overnight cooling of the grapes slows the ripening process, letting them develop complex flavors while retaining acidity.

The well-drained soils are predominantly made up of decomposed granite and red clay, perfect for the development of concentrated fruit. Less water in the ground means the vines will put more energy into the production of fruit, rather than foliage. The resultant wines have a more intense, concentrated flavor.

San Pasqual Valley AVA

The San Pasqual Valley AVA is an American Viticultural Area located north of the city of San Diego in southern California. The warm, dry climate is well-suited to the traditional Rhône grape varieties of Syrah, Mourvèdre and Viognier, as well as Merlot.

It was one of the first areas in California to be given AVA status, officially awarded in 1981. Today, there are just a handful of wine producers within the boundaries of San Pasqual Valley, with the larger South Coast AVA also pertinent to the area.

Located in a thin valley that runs inland from the city of Escondido, the wine region lies at a latitude of 33°N. This is further south than any European wine region, and is closer to the position of northern Morocco. The climate is dry and desert-like, with a long, hot summer that is followed by a mild winter.

The Pacific Ocean, 18 miles (28 kilometers) away, contributes cooling breezes to the San Pasqual Valley that increase its suitability for viticulture. These sweep into the vineyards in the afternoons, offering respite for the grapes after the intense morning sunlight. Colder nights extend the growing season, leading to the development of aromatics and varietal character in the grapes without sacrificing acidity.

The AVA has well-drained, granitic soils that lend themselves to the production of healthy vines. The low water content in the soil causes the vines to grow deep root systems to reach supplies lower in the ground.

Having less water also means the vines produce less energy-sapping foliage and instead pay more attention to growing small, concentrated berries with thick skins. The resultant wines have firm tannins and good structure.

San Luis Rey AVA

On August 30, 2024, the TTB (Alcohol and Tobacco Tax and Trade Bureau) of the United States approved the San Luis Rey American Viticultural Area (AVA). The new AVA is located in California's San Diego County, entirely within the previously established South Coast AVA. The AVA extends from the coastal city of Oceanside inland to the Merriman Mountains, Moosa Canyon and Fallbrook area. For that reason, the map in the Winery Maps & Resources section at the back of the book is titled Fallbrook-San Luis Rey AVA.

The area is named for the San Luis Rey River, which runs through the northern edge of the area and drains into the Pacific Ocean; and for Mission San Luis Rey—founded in 1798 and built close to the banks of the river. The defining characteristics of the San Luis Rey AVA include the area's topography, climate, and soil. These features are discussed below.

The San Luis Rey AVA sits at relatively low elevations (the mean elevation is 563 feet above sea level) and is located close to the Pacific Coastline. This situation allows cool ocean breezes to flow through the region, thus creating an overall cool, maritime climate. The average annual maximum temperature of the San Luis Rey AVA is significantly cooler than the surrounding areas (including the Temecula Valley AVA, San Pasqual Valley AVA, and Ramona Valley AVA).

Compared with the surrounding area, the bedrock supporting the San Luis Rey AVA is generally older and richer in sandy loam (an ideal texture for commercial viticulture, and a point of differentiation and potential advantage over much of the rest of the South Coast AVA). Soil parent materials include granite, sandstone and quartz.

The San Luis Rey AVA covers a total of approximately 97,733, with 256 acres currently planted to vineyards (with another 29 acres of planned vineyards). There are 44 commercial vineyards and just over 20 bonded wineries—located within the region. The leading grape varieties include Cabernet Sauvignon, Merlot, Cabernet Franc, Syrah, and Grenache.

San Diego County Wineries A to Z

Adobe Hill Winery

40740 Via Ranchitos Fallbrook CA 92028 760-444-0770 info@adobehill.com https://adobehillwinery.com/

Open: Wed. thru Sun. 12–Sunset.

Amenities: Events, Food, Music, Tasting, Wine Club.

Varietals: Cabernet Sauvignon, Merlot, Muscat Canelli, Pinot Grigio, Rose.

A hidden gem in Fallbrook's emerging wine scene, Adobe Hill Winery is where wine lovers become family. We're bringing fresh energy to San Diego County's wine country through organic, regenerative farming and a passion for crafting exceptional wines.

Alpenglow Winery

18011 Bluegrass Rd. Ramona CA 92065 760-504-1456 vino@alpenglowwinery.com https://www.alpenglowwinery.com/

Open: Sat. 11 am–5 pm. Reservations only for the other days.

Amenities: Food, Tasting.

Varietals: Albarino, Cabernet Sauvignon, Grenache, Merlot, Mourvèdre, Pinot Noir, Sauvignon Blanc, Syrah, Tempranillo.

A boutique winery on the west side of Ramona offering a selection of white, rose and red wine. Stop by our Ramona location to pick up wine direct from the tasting room.

Altipiano Vineyards

20365 Camino Del Aguila Escondido CA 92025 760-839-7999 altipianovineyardandwinery@gmail.com https://www.altipianovineyard.com

Open: Sat. & Sun. 12–6 pm.

Amenities: Tasting, Wine Club.

Varietals: Barbera, Merlot, Petite Sirah, Sangiovese.

Bring your friends and family to Altipiano Vineyard & Winery to learn about the wine-making process, taste some of our classic wines, and more.

Barrel 1 Winery

1007 Magnolia Avenue Ramona CA 92065 858-204-3144 info@barrel1.com
http://www.barrel1.com

Open: Sat. & Sun. 12–5 pm.

Amenities: Tasting, Wine Club.

Varietals: Cabernet Sauvignon, Merlot, Mourvèdre, Muscat Canelli, Tempranillo, Viognier.

After patiently waiting years for the vines to reach the right level of maturity and the wine to barrel age, the Cassidy's proudly opened the Barrel 1 tasting room in April 2015.

Bastian's Vineyards

15326 Bandy Canyon Rd. Escondido CA 92025 858-945-2405
bastiansvineyards@gmail.com http://bastiansvineyards.com

Open: Sat. & Sun. 12–5 pm.

Amenities: Events, Tasting.

Varietals: Merlot, Petite Sirah, Rose, Syrah, Viognier, Zinfandel.

Bastian's Vineyards is located in beautiful Highland Valley. We are a boutique winery with patio outdoor tasting areas. We currently offer 5 wines for tasting and most are estate wines.

Beach House Winery

1534 Sleeping Indian Rd. Oceanside CA 92058 760-732-3236
Info@BeachHouseWinery.com http://www.beachhousewinery.com

Open: Sat. & Sun. 12–4 pm. Reservations only.

Amenities: Tasting, Wine Club.

Varietals: Cabernet Sauvignon, Chardonnay, Grenache, Estate Cabernet Franc, Merlot, Sangiovese, Zinfandel.

Our passion is providing fine wines produced with time-honored processes to be enjoyed with family and friends. Cheers!

Belle Marie Winery

26312 Mesa Rock Road Escondido CA 92026 760-796-7557
https://www.bellemarie.com

Open: Mon. thru Sun. 11 am–5 pm.

Amenities: Events, Picnic, Tasting, Weddings, Wine Club.

Varietals: Barbera, Cabernet Franc, Cabernet Sauvignon, Chardonnay, Crescendo, Malbec, Petit Verdot, Rose, Sauvignon Blanc, Zinfandel.

Belle Marie Winery is a family-owned and operated boutique winery in Escondido situated on three and a half acres, with lush citrus groves and plenty of sunny and shaded areas throughout the grounds that are perfect to sit and relax with a glass of wine or enjoy a picnic or snack.

Bernardo Winery

13330 Paseo Del Verano Norte San Diego CA 92128 858-487-1866
sam@bernardowinery.com https://www.bernardowinery.com

Open: Wed. thru Sat. 11 am–8 pm, Sun. 11 am–6 pm.

Amenities: Events, Food, Music, Tasting, Weddings, Wine Club.

Varietals: Chardonnay, Petite Sirah, Syrah, Viognier, Zinfandel.

Originally opened in 1889 on what was part of a Spanish land grant, the Bernardo Winery has become, over the years, not only a fully productive San Diego winery, but a destination for wine lovers and tourism visitors alike since 1975.

Blue Door Winery, The

2608 B Street Julian CA 92036 (760) 765-0361
Kameron@thebluedoorwinery.com https://thebluedoorwinery.com/

Open: Mon. thru Sun. 12–5 pm weather permitting.

Amenities: Tasting, Wine Club.

Varietals: Barbera, Cabernet Franc, Cabernet Sauvignon, Merlot, Petit Verdot, Petite Syrah, Sangiovese, Sangria.

Come for a taste, a glass, or a bottle, you'll find knowledgeable and gracious hosts offering you interesting insight into our wines and the winemaking processes we employ.

Blue Honey Country Wines & Meads Co.

23719 Vista Ramona Rd. Ramona CA 92065 760-654-3103
BlueHoneyWM@gmail.com https://www.bluehoneywinesandmeads.com

Open: Thu. thru Sat. 11 am–7 pm, Sun. 12–5 pm. Reservations only.

Amenities: Tasting.

Varietals: Mead wines (made from honey) and non-grape Country Fruit Wines (made from blueberry, lemon, mango, peach, raspberry, strawberry fruit).

Located in beautiful Ramona, we are a micro-winery specializing in country wines (non-grape fruit wines) and meads (honey wine). Here at Blue Honey, we believe the fruits and honey are the stars of the show.

Brooking Vineyards

375 Skyline Drive Vista CA 92084 760-689-0160
https://www.brookingvineyards.com

Open: Most days 11 am–3 pm. Reservations only.

Amenities: Tasting, Wine Club.

Varietals: Barbera, Muscat Canelli Angelica, Tempranillo Angelica.

Brooking Vineyards is located in California's first wine region, San Diego County. Our climate is perfect for the traditional British style of winemaking. In California it became known as Angelica.

Buonvino Urban Winery

8680 Miralani Drive Suite 124 San Diego CA 92126 619-335-5419
buonvinowinery@gmail.com https://www.buonvino.us/

Open: Thu. 5:30–9:30 pm.

Amenities: Events, Tasting, Urban Winery/Wine Bar, Wine Club.

Varietals: Cabernet Sauvignon, Chardonnay, Moscato, Pinot Gris.

Whether you're a seasoned connoisseur or new to the world of wine, our knowledgeable staff will guide you through each pour, sharing insights into the winemaking process and the stories behind every bottle.

Burtech Family Vineyard (BFV)

1325 Pipeline Dr. Vista CA 92081 760-809-3461
info@burtechfamilyvineyard.com https://burtechfamilyvineyard.com

Open: Wed. thru Fri. 3–7 pm, Sat. 1–7 pm, Sun. 1–6 pm.

Amenities: Food, Tasting, Wine Club.

Varietals: Cabernet Franc, Cabernet Sauvignon, Chardonnay, Merlot, Petite Sirah, Pinot Gris, Pinot Noir, Rose, Sauvignon Blanc, Syrah.

We are happy to announce that our new location in Vista, is open. Come in and relax in our beautiful tasting room and enjoy a flight, glass, or bottle of your favorite BFV wine.

Cactus Star Vineyard

17029 Handlebar Rd. Ramona CA 92065 760-787-0779
info@CactusStarVineyard.com https://www.cactusstarvineyard.com

Open: We will be re-opening the tasting patio on Oct. 28th & Oct 29th, 2023; and then following the normal schedule of every 2nd and 4th weekend henceforward on Sat. & Sun. 1–4 pm, weather permitting. Reservations only.

Amenities: Tasting.

Varietals: Cabernet Sauvignon, Malbec, Petit Verdot, Tempranillo.

Cactus Star Vineyard is a boutique winery located on the west end of the Ramona Valley AVA. Our estate was established in 2001 with the first vintage crafted in 2004. We are one of the smallest wineries in Southern California producing 150 - 200 cases per year.

Campo Creek Vineyards

29556 Highway 94 Campo CA 91906 619-402-8733
campocreekvineyards@hotmail.com https://www.campocreekvineyards.com

Open: Reservations only.

Amenities: Tasting, Tours.

Varietals: Cabernet Sauvignon, Merlot, Syrah, Viognier, Zinfandel.

The handcrafted wines produced at Campo Creek reflect the friendly and rustic environment of the ranch, with exceptional value on the small batch wines, that include Cabernet Sauvignon, Merlot, Syrah, Viognier from the estate, and Zinfandel sourced from Potrero.

Carruth Cellars Urban Winery

3229 Roymar Rd. Oceanside CA 92058 858-847-9463
brandon@carruthcellars.com https://carruthcellars.com

Open: Mon. thru Thu. 3–8 pm, Fri. 3–10 pm, Sat. 12–10 pm, Sun. 12–8 pm.

Amenities: Events, Tasting, Wine Club.

Varietals: Cabernet Franc, Cabernet Sauvignon, Chardonnay, Malbec, Merlot, Pinot Noir, Rose, Sangiovese, Zinfandel.

We source quality grapes from premium vineyards in Northern California and transport them by truck to produce award winning wines by the beach. Experience our wines by the glass, in a tasting flight or to-go from one of our four locations in San Diego.

Casa Tiene Vista Winery

4150 Rock Mountain Rd. Fallbrook CA 92028 760-731-2356
susan@ctvvineyard.com https://www.yelp.com/biz/casa-tiene-vista-winery-fallbrook

Open: Sat. & Sun. 1–5 pm. Reservations only.

Amenities: Catering, Tasting.

Varietals: Cabernet, Chardonnay, Merlot, Pinot Grigio, Pinot Noir, Viognier.

Casa Tiene Vista is styled after the Old World European vineyards. The owners, Susan and Mick Gallagher, wanted to have a working vineyard, but we also wanted to have a park-like setting where their guests could find small nooks to sit and enjoy a glass of wine and the breathtaking views.

Castelli & Pizarro Family Winery

17872 Oak Grove Road Ramona CA 92065 619-997-5141 (Gate code needed, push # first and then 0011) info@castellifamilyvineyards.com
http://www.castellifamilyvineyards.com

Open: Sat. & Sun. 12–5:30 pm.

Amenities: Tasting, Wine Club.

Varietals: Barbera, Cabernet Franc, Cabernet Sauvignon, Chardonnay, Petit Verdot, Petite Sirah, Pinot Noir, Sangiovese, Syrah, Tempranillo, Viognier.

From hobby to 3,000 vines to underground wine cellar and award-winning wines, join your hosts in their Italian-style stucco, high ceiling and a large custom bar complemented by wines that include Pinot Noir, Syrah, Sangiovese, Cabernet Franc, Cabernet Sauvignon and Tempranillo varietals.

Charlie & Echo

8680 Miralani Drive #125 San Diego CA 92126 877-592-9095
info@charlieandecho.com https://charlieandecho.com

Open: Thu. & Fri. 4–8 pm, Sat. 1–8 pm, Sun. 1–6 pm.

Amenities: Events, Tasting, Wine Club.

Varietals: Lots of Blends, Desert Wines, Sangiovese, Sparling Wine.

We're an urban winery in San Diego producing natural, craft wine from local vineyards. We're on a mission to produce wines that exemplify San Diego's terroir, but its cuisine, culture, and lifestyle. We're small, independent, innovative, and care about everything we make.

Cheval Winery

2919 Hill Valley Drive Escondido CA 92028 760-690-6617
Cheers@ChevalWinery.com https://chevalwinery.com

Open: Fri. 4–7 pm, Sat. & Sun. 2–7 pm.

Amenities: Tasting, Wine Club.

Varietals: Barbera, Cabernet Franc, Cabernet Sauvignon, Grenache, Merlot, Syrah.

The owners, Donna and Dr. Randy Kaufman, were originally looking for a property for their champion show horses and stumbled upon this breath-taking location. They fell in love with the estate that just happened to come with a winery!

Chuparosa Vineyards

910 Gem Lane Ramona CA 92065 760-788-0059
carolyn@chuparosavineyards.com http://www.chuparosavineyards.com/

Open: Sat. & Sun. 11 am–5 pm.

Amenities: Tasting.

Varietals: Albarino, Cabernet Franc, Malbec, Sangiovese, Zinfandel.

Estate grown, produced and bottled reds (Zinfandel, Sangiovese, Malbec and Cabernet Franc) and a white (Albarino), with occasional limited production of vineyard-designated Ramona Valley treasures.

Coomber Craft Wines

611 Mission Ave. Oceanside CA 92054 760-231-8022
Sales@CoomberWines.com https://www.coomberwines.com

Open: Mon. thru Fri. 4–9 pm, Sat. & Sun. 12 – 9 pm.

Amenities: Events, Food, Music, Tasting, Wine Club.

Varietals: Cabernet Sauvignon, Chardonnay, Merlot, Muscat, Pinot Grigio, Pinot Noir, Sauvignon Blanc, Syrah.

In 2019, we were thrilled to open our Oceanside Urban Winery and Tasting Room, which has quickly become a favorite to locals and visitors alike. It is a comfortable and inviting establishment in the heart of Oceanside, and the ideal spot to spend a relaxing afternoon or evening among friends.

Cordiano Winery

15732 Highland Valley Rd. Escondido CA 92025 760-469-9463 x2
reservations@cordianowinery.com https://www.cordianowinery.com

Open: Wed. & Thu. 12–6 pm, Sat. & Sun. 12–7 pm. Reservations only.

Amenities: Events, Food, Tasting, Weddings, Wine Club.

Varietals: Barbera, Cabernet Franc, Chardonnay, Grenache, Merlot, Pinot Grigio, Sangiovese, Syrah, Tempranillo, Zinfandel.

Nestled in the hills of Highland Valley, you'll find Cordiano Winery, a family-owned and operated vineyard that takes pride in the craftsmanship of quality wines and of the labor practiced for ages in the old country.

Correcaminos Vineyard

1941 Lilac Road Ramona CA 92065 760-315-7444
info@correcaminosvineyard.com http://www.correcaminosvineyard.com

Open: Fri. thru Sun. 12–5 pm.

Amenities: Comedy, Tasting, Wine Club.

Varietals: Cabernet Sauvignon, Malbec, Syrah, Viognier, Zinfandel.

Located in Ramona, Correcaminos Vineyard makes beautifully, hand-crafted wines from estate and local grapes. Correcaminos, meaning Roadrunner, focuses on the nature of the rural Ramona lifestyle.

Costa Azul Winery

3195 Tyler St. Carlsbad CA 92008 619-752-4545 chrisvanalyea@gmail.com
costaazulwinery.com

Open: Mon., Tue. & Thu. 3–8 pm, Wed. & Fri. 3–9 pm, Sat. 2–8 pm, & Sun. 2–7 pm.

Amenities: Events, Music, Tasting, Urban Winery/Wine Bar, Wine Club.

Varietals: Albarino, Cabernet Sauvignon, Malbec, Merlot, Petite Sirah, Petit Verdot, Pinot Grigio, Pinot Noir, Riesling, Sangiovese, Sauvignon Blanc, Viognier.

Costa Azul Winery, located in Carlsbad, is a popular spot for wine tasting, with a variety of wines and a cozy atmosphere. Customers praise the friendly staff, especially servers like Jay, who provide excellent service and wine recommendations.

Coyote Oaks Vineyards

26312 Mesa Rock Road Escondido CA 92026 760-796-7557
Karen@coyoteoaksvineyards.com https://coyoteoaksvineyards.com

Open: Sat. & Sun. 11 am–5 pm at the Escondido Wine and Culinary Campus in the Hidden Valley Enoteca Chateau style castle.

Amenities: Tasting, Wine Club.

Varietals: Barbera, Cabernet Franc, Cabernet Sauvignon, Malbec, Montepulciano, Nebbiolo, Petit Verdot, Sangiovese, Tempranillo.

Coyote Oaks Vineyards is a Micro-Boutique Winery nestled among 300 year old oak trees that whisper the secrets of the coyote trodden paths. The sun-filled terroir has captured a unique moment in time that will make your taste buds howl in delight.

Crystal Hill Vineyard

24067 Old Julian Hwy. Ramona CA 92065 760-440-5229
swarner@crystalhillvineyard.com https://CrystalHillVineyard.com

Open: Fri. thru Sun. 12–6 pm. Reservations recommended.

Amenities: Food, Music, Tasting.

Varietals: Cabernet Franc, Cabernet Sauvignon, Chardonnay, Merlot, Petite Sirah, Pinot Gris, Sangiovese, Tempranillo.

Crystal Hill Vineyard is a San Diego County based producer of artisan, small-batch wines made from locally grown grapes including our vineyards in Ramona where you'll find us tending to our vines throughout the year.

Deerhorn Valley Vineyards

2516 Honey Springs Road Jamul CA 91935 619-468-0030
Robert@deerhornvalleyvineyards.co
https://www.facebook.com/deerhornvalleyvineyards/

Open: Sat. & Sun. 11 am–5 pm.

Amenities: Picnic, Tasting.

Varietals: Cabernet Franc, Cabernet Sauvignon, Chardonnay, Pinot Blanc, Pinot Noir, Rose, Sangiovese, Syrah, Zinfandel.

We are a small family run Boutique Winery located in beautiful Deerhorn Valley in the SE San Diego foothills below the iconic Lions Peak. We have our own vineyard on the property with 5 varietals bathed in the San Diego County sunshine.

Deer Park Winery & Auto Museum

29013 Champagne Boulevard Escondido CA 92026 760-749-1666
https://www.yelp.com/biz/deer-park-winery-and-auto-museum-escondido

Open: Mon. 10 am–5 pm, Thu. thru Sun. 10 am–5 pm.

Amenities: Tasting, Museum Tour.

Varietals: Chardonnay, Merlot, Petite Sirah, Sangiovese, Sauvignon Blanc, Sparkling, Zinfandel.

Deer Park annually produces and releases award-winning estate wines available for wine tasting weekends. It also had the world's largest Auto Museum of Convertibles & Americana, gift shop, vineyard, orchards, and lawns with shady oaks.

Domaine Artefact

15404 Highland Valley Rd. Escondido CA 92025 760-432-8034 Lynn@domaine-artefactwine.com http://domaine-artefactwine.com

Open: Sat. & Sun. 12–6 pm.

Amenities: Tasting, Wine Club.

Varietals: Grenache, Mourvèdre, Roussanne, Viognier.

Domaine Artefact is culmination and integration of our passion for wine, food, family and nature and a visit will provide a relaxing afternoon of winetasting, picnicking, wildlife viewing or strolling through native plantings, olive orchards and organic gardens.

Dulzura Vineyard & Winery

17323 Hwy. 94 Dulzura CA 91917 619-433-9896 https://dulzurawinery.com

Open: Fri. thru Sun. 12–6 pm in Summer and 5 pm in Winter.

Amenities: Lodging, Picnic, Tasting.

Varietals: Cabernet Franc, Cabernet Sauvignon, Chardonnay, Grenache, Malbec, Pinot Grigio, Riesling, Sauvignon Blanc, Viognier, Zinfandel.

The Dulzura Vineyard & Winery is located on the pioneer-era Clark Ranch, established in 1885. Today the ranch is still family owned. Come visit and share a glass of fine wine while enjoying the historical ambience and beauty of the Clark Ranch.

Edwards Vineyard & Cellars

26502 Hwy. 78 Ramona CA 92065 760-788-6800 edwardsvyd@aol.com https://www.edwardsvineyardandcellars.com/

Open: Sat. & Sun. 11 am–5 pm.

Amenities: Picnic, Tasting.

Varietals: Cabernet Sauvignon, Cuvee, Petite Sirah, Syrah.

The Edwards Family began producing commercial wines in the fall of 2004, however we planted our first Ramona Valley vineyard in 1990. Victor Edwards produced his first Petite Sirah in 1997, and it remains our family's flagship wine today.

Effenberger Vineyards

2347 Mountain View Dr. Escondido CA 92027 619-884-4542
roberta@effenbergervineyards.com https://www.effenbergervineyards.com

Open: Wine pick-up only after ordering wines online.

Amenities: Tasting (by local Pick-up only). Wine Club.

Varietals: Cabernet Sauvignon, Montepulciano, Sangiovese, Sagrantino, Syrah / Shiraz.

Our wines are handmade from estate fruit and carefully vetted vineyards. We're very small and passionate. We practice sustainable earth friendly farming, using no chemical fertilizers or herbicides, and use natural nutrition in the estate vineyard.

Emerald Creek Winery

38642 Highway 79 Warner Springs CA 92086 951-767-1391
info@emeraldcreekwinery.com https://emeraldcreekwinery.com

Open: Fri. thru Sun. 11 am–5 pm.

Amenities: Tasting, Tours, Weddings, Wine Club.

Varietals: Cabernet Franc, Cabernet Sauvignon, Chardonnay, Malbec, Merlot, Muscat Canelli, Pinot Grigio, Sparkling Wine, Syrah.

Emerald Creek Winery is located in Warner Springs on the North slope of Palomar Mountain. Our state of the art, expansive 5,000 square foot tasting room is fully furnished to allow our guests the ability to enjoy our hand-crafted artisan wines in a comfortable and relaxing environment.

Espinosa Vineyards

15360 Bandy Canyon Rd. Escondido CA 92025 619-772-0156
roberto@espwines.com https://www.espinosavineyards.com/

Open: Sat. & Sun. 12–5:30 pm.

Amenities: Picnic, Tasting.

Varietals: Albariño, Cabernet Sauvignon, Grenache, Rosé.

Our niche is balanced wine made from grapes that are native to Spain. We make 100% of our wines from grapes grown at our vineyard in Escondido and from grapes we buy, both locally and from some of the finest wine growing regions in California.

Estate d'Iacobelli

2175 Tecalote Dr. Fallbrook CA 92028 760-723-0616
vintner@estatediacobelli.com https://estatediacobelli.com

Open: Fri. thru Sun. 12–6 pm.

Amenities: Music, Tasting, Tours, Weddings, Wine Club.

Varietals: Cabernet Sauvignon, Moscato, Sangiovese, Viognier.

In the spring of 2013 Ronei and Lisa purchased a 15 acre estate in nearby Fallbrook. For Ronei and Lisa Iacobelli, making wine is part of their culture, upbringing and now, part of their daily lives.

Fallbrook Winery

2554 Via Rancheros Fallbrook CA 92028 760-728-0156 x 2
tastingroom@fallbrookwinery.com https://fallbrookwinery.com

Open: Mon. thru Wed. 10 am–4:30 pm, Thu. thru Sun. 10 am–6 pm.

Amenities: Tasting, Wine Club.

Varietals: Cabernet Franc, Cabernet Sauvignon, Grenache, Malbec, Merlot, Moscato, Petit Verdot, Sangiovese, Syrah.

A leader in California's emerging South Coast wine region, Fallbrook Winery's 36 acres rest between the Pacific Coast and the Pala Mesa Mountains, producing the highest quality red and white varietals.

Farquar Family Winery & Olive Oil

2839 Southern Oak Road Ramona CA 92065 858-335-1856
tsfarquar@gmail.com http://farquarfamilywinery.com/

Open: No tasting onsite. See website for off-site tasting events.

Amenities: Tasting off-site. Add your name and email, and check box, to join their email list on the Contact page of their website for news and updates about tasting venues.

Varietals: Cabernet Sauvignon, Rose, Roussanne, Sangiovese, Syrah, Zinfandel.

Sharing ideas with small production facilities has allowed us to acquire knowledge from the actual growers, millers, and wine makers. We look forward to sharing our wines and olive oil with you!

Forgotten Barrel Winery

1120 W. 15th Ave. Escondido CA 92025 888-620-8466
info@forgottenbarrel.com https://www.forgottenbarrel.com

Open: Thu. & Fri. 4–7 pm, Sat. & Sun. 12–6 pm.

Amenities: Food, Tasting, Weddings, Wine Club.

Varietals: Cabernet Sauvignon, Chardonnay, Mourvèdre, Port, Sangiovese, Syrah, Tannat, Viognier, Zinfandel.

Forgotten Barrel Winery offers a wide selection of premium hand crafted wines using fruit sourced from Napa, Sonoma, Central Coast and San Diego County by our winemaker John Eppler, having worked in Napa for Robert Mondavi, Rosenblum Cellars, and his own brand, John Robert Eppler Wines.

Gianni Buonomo Vintners

4836 Newport Ave. San Diego CA 92107 562-458-9477 info@GBVintners.com
https://www.gbvintners.com

Open: Wed. thru Sat. 1–7 pm.

Amenities: Tasting, Wine Club.

Varietals: German and Italian blends.

On site we produce rare, under-appreciated varietals that are definitely not part of the American mainstream.

Grafted Cellars Winery

2379 La Mirada Dr. Vista CA 92081 760-295-6612 info@graftedcellars.com
https://graftedcellarswinery.com/locations/grafted-cellars-winery/

Open: Thu. 4–9 pm, Fri. 3–9 pm, Sat. 1–9 pm, Sun. 1–7 pm.

Amenities: Events, Food, Picnic, Tasting, Urban Winery/Wine Bar, Wine Club.

Varietals: Barbera, Cabernet Franc, Cabernet Sauvignon, Chardonnay, Chenin Blanc, Grenache, Merlot, Moscato, Pinot Noir, Rose, Sangiovese, Sauvignon Blanc, Syrah, Viognier, Zinfandel.

A family-owned Urban Winery and Tasting Room, we source our grapes from right here in Vista, to Napa Valley, to Oregon's Willamette Valley, any American Viticultural Areas (AVAs) in between…but quality varietals from our own South Coast AVA are a priority, to showcase our local terroir and potential.

Granite Lion Cellars

2801 Jamul Highlands Rd. Jamul CA 91935 619-669-2982
glc@granitelioncellars.com http://www.granitelioncellars.com

Open: Mon. thru Fri. 11 am–5 pm, Sat. & Sun. 11 am–5 pm.

Amenities: Food, Tasting, Tours, Wine Club.

Varietals: Cabernet Sauvignon, Chardonnay, Marsanne, Merlot, Pinot Gris, Riesling, Rose, Sauvignon Blanc, Sparkling Wine, Syrah, Viognier, Zinfandel.

Granite Lion Cellars prioritizes environmentally conscious practices to minimize our impact on the planet, while producing high-quality wines. Careful care of our vineyard is essential for winemaking, each step contributes to the flavor, aroma, balance, and overall character of the wine.

Hatfield Creek Vineyards & Winery

1625 Highway 78 Ramona CA 92065 760-787-1102
elaine@hatfieldcreekvineyards.com http://www.hatfieldcreekvineyards.com

Open: Fri. thru Sun. 11 am–5 pm.

Amenities: Events, Food, Tasting, Wine Club.

Varietals: Cabernet Sauvignon, Petite Sirah, Sangiovese, Syrah, Zinfandel.

Scenic boutique winery and vineyards. Specializing on award winning big, bold, dark, dry red wines. Vineyards produce Zinfandel, Petite Sirah & Malbec grapes for Estate wines. Other varietals from local Ramona Valley AVA vineyards include Syrah, Sangiovese, and Cabernet Sauvignon.

Hawk Watch Winery

27054 Chihuahua Valley Rd. Warner Springs CA 92086 951-326-0698
Hawkwatchwinery@gmail.com https://hawkwatchwinery.com

Open: Fri. thru Sun. 10 am–5 pm.

Amenities: Picnic, Tasting, Wine Club.

Varietals: Cabernet Franc, Cabernet Sauvignon, Malbec, Merlot, Petit Verdot, Petite Sirah, Rose, Sangiovese, Sauvignon Blanc, Syrah, Viognier, Zinfandel.

Our wines are hand-crafted from only the finest fruit using hands-on, old world wine making techniques. Each bottle truly represents the excitement and enthusiasm we have for premium wine making, and the passion and obsession we have for viticulture.

Highland Valley Vineyards

15412 Bandy Canyon Road Escondido CA 92025 858-531-6589
info@highlandvalleyvineyards.com https://www.highlandvalleyvineyards.com

Open: Sat. & Sun. 12–6 pm (5 pm in Winter).

Amenities: Tasting, Wine Club.

Varietals: Barbera, Malbec, Sauvignon Blanc, Zinfandel.

Welcome to Highland Valley Vineyards, a boutique micro winery perched on the edge of beautiful Highland Valley and San Pasqual Valley in the San Diego foothills. We grow Bordeaux variety grapes and together with other fruit carefully selected, we hand style robust red wines.

Hillside Ranch Vineyard

14169 Hillside Drive Jamul CA 91935 info@hillsideranchvineyard.com
https://hillsideranchvineyard.com/

Open: Reservations only.

Amenities: Events, Lodging, Tasting, Weddings.

Varietals: Sauvignon Blanc, Syrah, Pinot Noir, Viognier.

The well-draining granite soil, the cool off shore breezes, and the long sunny days are ideal conditions for growing grapes. With the help of wine growing consultants, Grant Spotts and Sarah Babine, two and half acres of formerly arid, rocky land have been converted to a flourishing vineyard.

Hill Top Winery

30801 Valley Center Road Valley Center CA 92082 858-405-9314
info@hilltopwinery.com https://hilltopwinery.com

Open: Thu. thru Sun. 12–8 pm.

Amenities: Events, Food, Tasting, Weddings, Wine Club.

Varietals: Barbera, Cabernet Franc, Cabernet, Merlot, Zinfandel.

More than just a Winery, Hilltop Winery is a destination. With Beautiful scenery surrounding its new Tasting Room and Gourmet Mobile Kitchen, this Winery is the perfect backdrop for your Wedding, Anniversary, Birthday and more!

Hungry Hawk Vineyards & Winery

3255 Summit Dr. Escondido CA 92025 760-489-1758
info@hungryhawkvineyards.com https://www.hungryhawkvineyards.com

Open: Reservations recommended. Thu. 2–7 pm, Thu. 12–7 pm, Sat. & Sun. 12–6 pm.

Amenities: Events, Music, Tasting, Tours, Wine Club.

Varietals: Cabernet Sauvignon, Mourvèdre, Petite Sirah, Port, Rose, Sauvignon Blanc.

This winery's premium craftsmanship, limited production boutique winery, has a unique style that granted its recognition as one of the best San Diego wineries by many locals. Founded by Jeannine and Ed Embly in 2014, this ten-acre estate produces 15 varietals of grapes.

Keys Creek Winery

27118 N. Broadway Escondido CA 92026 760-615-3640
Info@keyscreekwinery.com https://www.keyscreekwinery.com/

Open: Fri. 5:30–7:30 pm, Sat. 1 – 5 pm.

Amenities: Tasting, Wine Club.

Varietals: Cabernet Sauvignon, Muscat Canelli, Petite Syrah, Sangiovese, Syrah, Tannat, Zinfandel.

Visit Keys Creek Winery to taste our hand crafted wine and experience the transformation from vineyard to your glass. Our outdoor, oak shaded tasting area is a quiet and peaceful place to fully enjoy some of North San Diego County's best wine.

Kohill Winery

17211 Highlander Drive Ramona CA 92065 760-787-1042 mike@kohill.com
https://californiawinenavigator.com/business-directory/kohill-winery

Open: Sat. & Sun. 12–5 pm.

Amenities: Tasting.

Varietals: Cabernet Sauvignon, Sauvignon Blanc, Viognier.

Our intimate tasting room hosts a magnificent collection of boutique vintages to be enjoyed at our charming wine bar or outdoor patio overlooking Ramona's majestic Valley of the Sun.

Koi Zen Cellars Craft Winery

12225 World Trade Drive San Diego CA 92128 858-381-2675
wine@koizencellars.com https://koizencellars.com

Open: Reservations required for Fri. to Sun. Wed. & Thu. 3–8 pm, Fri. 3–9 pm, Sat. 1–9 pm, Sun. 1–6 pm.

Amenities: Tasting, Wine Club.

Varietals: Cabernet Sauvignon, Chardonnay, Merlot, Petit Verdot, Petite Sirah, Sauvignon Blanc, Sparkling Wine, Syrah, Viognier, Zinfandel.

Good wine indeed starts in the vineyard, and therefore we only source grapes from the very best vineyards and locations. Then with tender loving care, we bring the fruit as whole clusters to our winery and this is where the magic begins.

La Costa Wine Co.

7750 El Camino Real Suite L Carlsbad CA 92009 760-431-8455
wine@lacostawineco.com https://www.lacostawineco.com/

Open: Mon. thru Thu. 11 am–9 pm, Fri. 11 am–10 pm, Sat. 11 am–9 pm, Sun. 11 am–6 pm.

Amenities: Events, Food, Tasting, Tours, Urban Winery/Wine Bar, Wine Club.

Varietals: Merlot, Moscato, Pinot Noir, Riesling, and large assortment of blends.

We are a passionate group of wine drinkers who feel that discovering and drinking good wine should be both easy and compelling, without any sense of intimidation or pretension. Above all, drinking good wine should be inspiring and fun!

La Serenissima Vineyards & Winery

35168 Hwy. 79 Warner Springs CA 92086 951-326-0205 info@vinotiso.com https://vinotiso.com/

Open: Everyday by appointment only.

Amenities: Tasting, Tours, Wine Club.

Varietals: Cabernet Franc, Cabernet Sauvignon, Merlot, Pinot Grigio, Syrah.

Both owning and directly operating our boutique winery, we are able to give great attention to every stage of the process in order to produce wines that are known for their expression, complexity and elegance.

Little Oaks Winery

6084 Corte Del Cedro #105 Carlsbad CA 92011 760-494-0597 x 19 info@littleoakswinery.com https://www.littleoakswinery.com

Open: Varies. Reservations only.

Amenities: Tasting, Wine Club.

Varietals: Barbera, Malbec, Rose, Sangiovese, Syrah / Shiraz, Viognier.

Little Oaks Winery is a small, urban winery that is family owned and operated in Carlsbad. We source our grapes locally from the highest quality vineyards in San Diego county. Our limited production allows us to focus on creating quality over quantity.

LJ Crafted Wines

5621 La Jolla Boulevard San Diego CA 92037 858-551-8890 lowell@ljcraftedwines.com https://www.ljcraftedwines.com

Open: Tue. thru Thu. 4–9 pm, Fri. 4–9:30 pm, Sat. 2–9:30 pm.

Amenities: Tasting, Wine Club.

Varietals: Albarino, Chardonnay, Chenin Blanc, Malbec, Petit Verdot, Pinot Noir, Sangiovese, Sauvignon Blanc, Syrah, Zinfandel.

An urban winery tasting room serving small batch wines made in Napa Valley directly from the barrel into re-usable bottles. Supporting a zero-waste lifestyle.

Mahogany Mountain Vineyard & Winery

14905 Mussey Grade Rd. Ramona CA 92065 760-788-7048
info@mahoganymountain.com http://www.mahoganymountain.com

Open: Varies. Reservations only.

Amenities: Events, Tasting.

Varietals: Cabernet Sauvignon, Merlot, Mourvèdre, Syrah.

We are a small, family-owned and operated winery specializing in limited production of handcrafted estate premium wines: Barbera, Cabernet Sauvignon, Malbec, Merlot, Mourvèdre, Muscat Canelli, Petit Verdot, Syrah, Zinfandel, Burgundy-style blends, Rhone-style blends and Port-style wines.

Menghini Winery Inc.

1150 Julian Orchards Dr. Julian CA 92036 760-765-2072
grapes@menghiniwinery.com
https://californiawineryadvisor.com/winery/Menghini-Winery/

Open: Mon. thru Fri. 11 am–4 pm, Sat. & Sun. 11 am–5 pm.

Amenities: Tasting.

Varietals: Cabernet Sauvignon, Riesling, Sauvignon Blanc, Syrah.

We are the second oldest winery in San Diego County and the oldest in Julian. The winery is surrounded by apple orchards and a six acre vineyard. We have expansive picnic grounds with gorgeous 365 degree views of the countryside.

Mermaid Valley Vineyard

18420 Highland Valley Road Ramona CA 92065 760-315-9011
mermaidvineyard@gmail.com http://mermaidvalleyvineyard.com

Open: Sat. 11 am–5 pm. Reservations only for other days.

Amenities: Tasting.

Varietals: Malbec, Merlot, Petite Sirah, Sauvignon Blanc, Syrah, Viognier, Zinfandel.

Mermaid Valley Vineyard is a current member of the Ramona Valley Vineyard Association and the San Diego County Vintners Association and would love for you to come taste for yourself the wonderful wines of Mermaid Valley Vineyard.

Mia Marie Vineyards

15036 Highland Valley Road Escondido CA 92025 760-215-9132
https://miamarie.com

Open: Fri. 2–8 pm, Sat. 12–8 pm, Sun. 12–7 pm.

Amenities: Food, Music, Tasting, Wine Club.

Varietals: Cabernet Sauvignon, Malbec, Merlot, Mourvèdre, Sangiovese, Sauvignon Blanc, Tempranillo.

Sitting on 105 acres overlooking scenic Highland Valley in San Diego County, Mia Marie strives to deliver a variety of craft wines in a relaxed setting. Family owned and operated, we cultivate our grapes and make our wine with a dedication to quality.

Milagro Winery

18750 Littlepage Rd. Ramona CA 92065 760-787-0738
alex@milagrowinery.com https://www.milagrowinery.com

Open: Sat. & Sun. 12–6 pm.

Amenities: Events, Tasting, Weddings, Wine Club.

Varietals: Barbera, Cabernet Sauvignon, Chardonnay, Merlot, Pinot Gris, Rose, Sangiovese, Sauvignon Blanc.

Our commitment to working in harmony with our land is at the core of everything we do. We cultivate our grapes, craft our wines, and farm our soil with integrity, authenticity, and a desire to honor the rich characteristics unique to our Ramona Valley.

Mission Cellars Urban Winery

14053 Midland Rd. Poway CA 92064 858-829-0444 info@missioncellars.net
https://www.yelp.com/biz/mission-cellars-poway-2

Open: Tue. thru Thu. 3–8 pm, Fri. 3–9 pm, Sat. 11 am–9 pm, Sun. 12–7pm.

Amenities: Events, Tasting, Tours, Wine Club.

Varietals: Cabernet Sauvignon, Chardonnay, Malbec, Petite Sirah, Pinot Blanc, Pinot Gris, Rose, Sangiovese.

Opened July 2018, Mission Cellars began crafting exquisite wine and experiences right in the heart of Poway to harvest the grapes from the Oregon and California wine countries. White and red grapes are harvested by hand at their optimal maturity levels, to provide the highest quality wine possible.

Monserate Vineyards & Winery

2757 Gird Rd. Fallbrook CA 92028 760-268-9625
wineclub@monseratewinery.com https://monseratewinery.com

Open: Wed. thru Sat. 11 am–6 pm, Sun. & Mon. 11 am–6 pm.

Amenities: Events, Food, Tasting, Weddings, Wine Club.

Varietals: Barbera, Grenache, Montepulciano, Zinfandel and many unique blends.

Today, Monserate Winery boasts breathtaking vineyards, tranquil lakes and spectacular scenery. As our winery continues to grow and expand our operations near San Diego, we stay true to our original vision.

Myrtle Creek Vineyards

1600 Via Vista Fallbrook CA 92028 442-444-5066
contact@myrtlecreekvineyards.com https://www.myrtlecreekvineyards.com

Open: Sat. & Sun. 12–5 pm.

Amenities: Events, Tasting, Wine Club.

Varietals: Albarino, Cabernet Franc, Cabernet Sauvignon, Rose, Sangiovese, Sauvignon Blanc, Syrah.

Myrtle Creek Vineyards is a family-run boutique winery making quality, hand-crafted wines in small batches. Most of our grapes are grown right here in our own vineyard, then picked by hand.

Negociant Winery

1263 University Ave. San Diego CA 92103 619-535-1747
info@negociantwinery.com https://www.negociantwinery.com/

Open: Wed. & Thu. 4–9:30 pm, Fri. & Sat. 4–10 pm., Sun. 12–4 pm.

Amenities: Events, Tasting, Urban Winery/Wine Bar, Wine Club.

Varietals: Albarino, Cabernet Sauvignon, Grenache, Malbec, Petite Sirah, Pinot Noir, Rose, Roussanne, Sauvignon Blanc, Tempranillo, Viognier.

Nestled in the heart of San Diego's vibrant Hillcrest neighborhood, Negociant Winery is an urban winery and tasting room dedicated to crafting small-batch wines with big personality.

Oddish Wine

5322 Banks Street San Diego CA 92110 858-205-1328 billy@oddish.wine
https://www.oddish.wine

Open: Wed. 4–8 pm, Thu. & Fri. 4–9 pm, Sat. 12–9:30 pm, Sun. 12–8 pm.

Amenities: Food, Music, Tasting, Wine Club.

Varietals: Tempranillo and fruity wines.

We make minimal intervention wine and as much as possible we try to use minimal intervention practices with responsibly farmed grapes from San Diego County.

Old Julian Vineyards & Winery

25352 Old Julian Hwy. Ramona CA 92065 949-374-7700
shelli.oldjulianvineyards@gmail.com http://oldjulianvineyards.com

Open: Fri. thru Sun. 12–6 pm.

Amenities: Music, Tasting.

Varietals:, Cabernet Franc, Cabernet Sauvignon, Merlot, Petit Verdot, Petite Sirah, Rose, Sauvignon Blanc, Syrah, Viognier.

Old Julian Vineyards & Winery is a renowned vineyard winery and Brandy maker known for its iconic Red Barn. We are a Brother/Sister team that continually features a variety of high-quality and affordable wines and brandy.

Old Survey Vineyards

16850 Old Survey Rd. Escondido CA 92025 760-480-7232
http://www.oldsurveyvineyards.com

Open: Fri. 2 pm–Sunset, Sat. & Sun. 11 am–Sunset.

Amenities: Tasting.

Varietals: Barbera, Grenache, Mourvèdre, Pinot Grigio.

We are a small family owned Winery overlooking the San Pasqual Valley established in 2008.

Orfila Vineyards & Winery

13455 San Pasqual Rd. Escondido CA 92025 760-738-6500 mike@orfila.com
http://www.orfila.com

Open: Daily 11 am–7 pm.

Amenities: Tasting, Tours, Wine Club.

Varietals: Chardonnay, Merlot, Pinot Gris, Pinot Noir, Riesling, Rose, Sangiovese, Sauvignon Blanc, Sparkling Wine, Syrah.

Orfila produces critically acclaimed wines using Italian and French varietals, including those from the Rhône Valley, Burgundy and Bordeaux. We source our grapes from both the estate and select vineyards from Sonoma, San Luis Obispo, and Santa Barbara Counties.

Pali Wine Co.

2130 India Street San Diego CA 92101 619-569-1300 littleitaly@paliwineco.com
https://www.opentable.com/r/pali-wine-co-little-italy-tasting-room-san-diego

Open: Mon. & Tue. 4–9 pm, Wed. & Thu. 4–10 pm, Fri. 1 pm–12 am, Sat. 11 am–12 am, Sun. 11 am–9 pm.

Amenities: Events, Food, Music, Tasting, Urban Winery/Wine Bar.

Varietals: Cabernet Sauvignon, Chardonnay, Grenache, Merlot, Petite Sirah, Pinot Noir, Rose, Sparkling.

The family-owned winery highlights the diversity and nuanced qualities of the California Central Coast wine-growing area. From our Pali Pinot Noirs & Chardonnays, to our Tower 15 bold, nuanced wines, and Neighborhood zippy, natural cuvées, our three wine labels are sure to please any pallet.

Pamo Valley Vineyards & Winery

636 Main Street Ramona CA 92065 760-271-3090 jenniferlane127@yahoo.com
http://pamovalleywinery.com

Open: Mon. thru Thu. 2–6 pm, Fri. & Sat. 2–8 pm, Sun. 12–5 pm.

Amenities: Tasting.

Varietals: Barbera, Cabernet Franc, Cabernet Sauvignon, Chardonnay, Merlot, Petite Sirah, Rose, Sangiovese, Syrah, Tempranillo, Viognier, Zinfandel.

At Pamo Valley Winery, we are very passionate about making premium wines that are pleasing to the palate. We believe that wine is feminine by its very nature. Wine is a gift from Mother Nature. When crafted by capable human hands, and well made, it is a joy.

Pauma Vista Vineyard

29431 Cole Grade Road Valley Center CA 92082 760-644-4432
paumavistavineyard@gmail.com https://www.paumavistavineyard.com/

Open: Fri. thru Sun. 12–6 pm.

Amenities: Tasting, Wine Club.

Varietals: Cabernet Sauvignon, Chardonnay, Grenache, Petite Sirah, Rose, Sauvignon Blanc, Zinfandel.

In 2018, they purchased a 7-acre plot, planted in less than one year, and currently concentrating on farming Spanish and Rhone varietals including Petite Sirah, Tempranillo, Grenache, Mourvèdre, Syrah and Albarino grapes.

Pearson Brothers Winery

7123 Dehesa Rd. El Cajon CA 92019 619-370-4507
pearsonbrotherswinery@gmail.com https://www.pearsonbroswinery.com

Open: Sat. & Sun. 12–6 pm.

Amenities: Tasting, Tours, Weddings, Wine Club.

Varietals: Fruity honey wines.

We artfully blend local wildflower honey, Valencia orange, and Indonesian vanilla resulting in a smooth delicious white honey wine with decadent floral and citrus aromas. The wine starts slightly sweet, and then cascades into a complex dance of flavors.

Poco Montana Vineyards

23136 Vista Ramona Rd. Ramona CA 92065 760-996-7853
daniel@pocomontana.com https://pocomontana.com/

Open: Sat. 1–6 pm. Reservations only.

Amenities: Events, Tasting.

Varietals: Albarino, Malbec, Merlot, Petite Sirah, Primitivo, Rose.

Nestled in the rolling hills of Ramona, Poco Montaña Vineyards is one of the region's newest wineries, specializing in handcrafted, small batch estate wines and the production of wines from grapes grown in the Ramona Valley AVA.

Poppaea Vineyard

25643 Old Julian Hwy. Ramona CA 92065 858-357-1741
poppaeasabina13@gmail.com https://poppaeavineyard.com/

Open: Fri. 2–5 pm, Sat. & Sun. 12–6 pm.

Amenities: Tasting.

Varietals: Barbera, Montepulciano, Nebbiolo, Primitivo, Sagrantino, Sangiovese.

The first plantings of grape vines at Poppaea took place in 2010. The family selected 6 Italian red varietals to work with: Sangiovese, Montepulciano, Nebbiolo, Barbera, Primitivo and Sagrantino.

Principe di Tricase Winery

18425 Highland Valley Rd. Ramona CA 92065 760-315-8872
wine@pineandwine.com http://www.pineandwine.com

Open: Reservations only.

Amenities: Food, Private Events, Tasting, Wine Club.

Varietals: Cabernet Franc, Cabernet Sauvignon, Chardonnay, Malbec, Merlot, Sauvignon Blanc, Syrah, Zinfandel plus many Italian estate varietals.

We produce only Natural Wines, using only local grapes. We grow 13 different estate varietals, mostly the Italian ones, and we source other 8 from local growers with whom we built a trustful and strong relationship over the years.

Propaganda Wine Co.

2129 Industrial Ct. Vista CA 92081 858-255-4421 Info@propagandawines.com https://propagandawines.com/

Open: Mon. 4–8 pm, Tue. thru Fri. 4–10 pm, Sat. 11 am–10 pm, Sun. 11 am–8 pm.

Amenities: Comedy, Music, Tasting, Wine Club.

Varietals: Cabernet Sauvignon, Grenache, Petite Sirah, Pinot Noir, Viognier.

Our goal is to produce the most enjoyable wines possible and have damn good time doing it. We want wine to be more approachable and welcome everyone to the process. It's not just a beverage for the aristocrats, but a tasty libation that can be enjoyed by all, nobles and proletariat alike.

Quigley Fine Wines

1551 Fourth Ave. Ste. 101 San Diego CA 92101 619-795-7043 info@quigleyfinewines.com https://quigleyfinewines.com/

Open: Tue. thru Sat. 4–9 pm.

Amenities: Events, Tasting, Urban Winery/Wine Bar, Wine Club.

Varietals: Cabernet Franc, Cabernet Sauvignon, Chardonnay, Grenache, Malbec, Merlot, Petite Sirah, Pinot Grigio, Pinot Noir, Riesling, Rose, Sauvignon Blanc, Syrah, Tempranillo, Zinfandel.

Comfortable and welcoming, the space offers clients the opportunity to taste the boutique wines of Europe, Australia, and New Zealand that are carried exclusively through Quigley Fine Wines—as well as wines crafted by top California and Oregon winemakers.

Ramona Ranch Winery

23578 Highway 78 Ramona CA 92065 760-789-1622 teri@ramonaranch.com http://www.ramonaranchwines.com

Open: Fri. thru Sun. 11 am–6 pm.

Amenities: Picnic, Tasting, Wine Club.

Varietals: Merlot, Sauvignon Blanc, Syrah, Tannat.

Our wines are produced from Estate and local Ramona vineyards that we have personally selected for the quality fruit due to the meticulous attention of each grower. You can taste the care and commitment to the land in every glass of our award winning wines.

Rancho Guejito Vineyard

17224 San Pasqual Valley Rd. Escondido CA 92027 800-677-8887
info@ranchoguejitovineyard.com https://www.ranchoguejitovineyard.com

Open: Sat. & Sun. 11 am–7 pm (or earlier at Dusk in Winter).

Amenities: Events, Food, Tasting, Tours, Weddings, Wine Club.

Varietals: Chardonnay, Grenache, Mourvèdre, Rose, Roussanne, Viognier.

Our wines are carefully crafted from grapes grown with care and consideration by our master winemaker, Chris Broomell. Here, you will find all of our wines, including our latest releases that can be enjoyed now or cellared to continue to improve with each season.

Rancho San Martin

17249 Sundance Dr. Ramona CA 92065 760-650-6851
ginny.rsmwinery@gmail.com http://rsmwines.com

Open: Sat. & Sun. 12–5 pm.

Amenities: Tasting.

Varietals: Cabernet Sauvignon, Grenache, Sangiovese, Tempranillo.

Come visit and enjoy our Italian and Spanish varietals, selected to match our terroir and climate. Relax in the quiet country atmosphere and taste our wine that has been barrel aged for 2 1/2 plus years. Our mission is for you to have the best wine tasting experience in the valley.

Rashelica Winery & Art Garden

17948 Hwy 67 Ramona CA 92065 Chat Online
https://www.rashelicagarden.com/

Open: Sat. & Sun. 11 am–6 pm. Reservations only.

Amenities: Food, Tasting, Weddings.

Varietals: Cabernet, Franc, Malbec, Petite Sirah.

Rashelica Winery & Art Garden is a cultural destination nestled in the hills of Ramona Valley. Rashelica offers guests an experience unlike any other; complete with award-winning handcrafted wines, an extensive collection of world-class sculptures, and live performances by local musicians.

Record Family Wines

1035 University Ave. San Diego CA 92103 619-759-0153
info@recordfamilywines.com https://www.recordfamilywines.com

Open: Wed. thru Fri. 4–9 pm, Sat. 1–8 pm, Sun. 1–6 pm.

Amenities: Tasting.

Varietals: Cabernet Sauvignon, Syrah, Viognier.

Planted to Cabernet Sauvignon, Grenache, Sauvignon Blanc and Viognier vines, we choose the best fruit our vineyard produces each year to bottle under our label. Our intention is to create wines that are representative of the place the grapes come from.

Reds Whites and Brews

629 Main Street Ramona CA 92065 619-517-2131
info@redswhitesandbrews.wine http://www.redswhitesandbrews.wine

Open: Mon. 5–9 pm, Wed. & Thu. 4–10 pm, Fri. 3–11 pm, Sat. 3–11 pm, Sun. 1–7 pm.

Amenities: Events, Tasting, including Beer and Cider tasting.

Varietals: Albarino, Cabernet Sauvignon, Chardonnay, Rose, Sangiovese, Syrah, Viognier, Zinfandel.

Welcome to Reds Whites and Brews in the heart of Old Town Ramona! We are so lucky to be a part of this wonderful community. We serve craft beer, Ramona wine, and local cider, creating a welcoming environment for everyone over the age of 21.

Rock Canyon Vineyards

3355 Emmanuel Way Alpine CA 91901 619-445-4763 rockcanyon@hughes.net
https://rockcanyonvineyards.com

Open: Appointment only.

Amenities: Lodging, Tasting, Tours.

Varietals: Cabernet Sauvignon, Sangiovese, Syrah, Tempranillo, Zinfandel.

Although we grow several varieties, we strive to find old vine (mature) grapes throughout Southern California to produce a mature, full bodied, delicious wine. We have discontinued our commercial operations, but we still enjoy producing wine for family and friends.

Rose's Tasting Room

2754 Calhoun St. San Diego CA 92110 619-293-7673
info@rosestastingroom.com https://rosestastingroom.com/#

Open: Mon. thru Fri. 11 am–9 pm, Sat. & Sun. 10 am–9 pm.

Amenities: Tasting, Urban Winery/Wine Bar.

Varietals: Moscato, Rose, other Reds.

As a native San Diegan Julie wanted to promote San Diego so Rose's pours beer & wine produced locally. We buy craft beer & boutique wine from other family-owned businesses. Whenever possible we strive to purchase items made in San Diego County.

Rustic Ridge Vineyards

15262 Lyons Valley Road Jamul CA 91935 619-251-7115
https://www.rusticridgevineyards.com/

Open: Sat. & Sun. 11 am–6 pm (Summer hours). Reservations recommended.

Amenities: Events, Food, Lodging, Picnic, Tasting, Wine Club.

Varietals: Cabernet Sauvignon, Malbec, Pinot Gris, Pinot Noir, Rose, Syrah, Zinfandel.

We select our grapes from the best regions of California to produce our excellent wines. Enjoy a selection of snacks, a picnic basket charcuterie, warm pretzels and chocolate chip cookies and pizzas.

San Pasqual Winery – La Mesa Boulevard

8364 La Mesa Boulevard La Mesa CA 91942 619-462-1797
info@sanpasqualwinery.com https://www.sanpasqualwinery.com/Homepage

Open: Mon. thru Thu. 1–8 pm, Fri. thru Sat. 1–10 pm, Sun. 12–5 pm.

Amenities: Events, Tasting, Urban Winery/Wine Bar, Wine Club.

Varietals: Barbera, Cabernet Franc, Cabernet Sauvignon, Chardonnay, Merlot, Moscato, Petit Verdot, Petite Sirah, Riesling, Sparkling Wine, Syrah, Tempranillo.

San Pasqual Winery is a small, family owned winery located in La Mesa (with two other tasting rooms), about 15 miles east of San Diego. The winery was later "reinvented" as San Diego's first urban winery, earning it a spot on Sunset Magazine's list of "Hot 100 West Coast Trends."

San Pasqual Winery – La Mesa Wine Works

8167 Center St. La Mesa CA 91942 619-741-0700 info@lamesawineworks.com
https://lamesawineworks.com/

Open: Thu. 3–8 pm, Fri. 3–9 pm, Sat. 12–9 pm, Sun. 12–5 pm.

Amenities: Events, Tasting, Urban Winery/Wine Bar, Wine Club.

Varietals: Chardonnay, Malbec, Petite Sirah, Sparkling, Zinfandel.

Their winery namesake was the San Pasqual Winery that dates to the 1970's when it was located in the San Pasqual Valley. Later, the winery "reinvented" itself as San Diego's first urban winery, earning it a spot on Sunset Magazine's list of "Hot 100 West Coast Trends."

San Pasqual Winery – Seaport Village

805 West Harbor Drive Suite A San Diego CA 92101 619-544-9463
info@sanpasqualwinery.com https://www.sanpasqualwinery.com/Seaport-Village-San-Diego--Tasting-Room

Open: Mon. thru Sun. 10 am–9 pm.

Amenities: Events, Tasting, Tours, Urban Winery/Wine Bar, Wine Club.

Varietals: Albarino, Cabernet Franc, Cabernet Sauvignon, Chardonnay, Malbec, Merlot, Moscato, Petite Sirah, Syrah, Tempranillo.

The original winery was located in the San Pasqual Valley, however, the winery was later "reinvented" as San Diego's first urban winery, earning it a spot on Sunset Magazine's list of "Hot 100 West Coast Trends."

Sblendorio Winery

38973 De Luz Rd. Fallbrook CA 92028 714-421-3294
info@sblendoriowinery.com http://www.sblendoriowinery.com

Open: Reservations only.

Amenities: Picnic, Tasting, Tours.

Varietals: Barbera, Cabernet Sauvignon, Mourvèdre, Siano, Treviano.

We are a boutique winery that produces wines from vineyards of distinction. All our wines are vineyard designated, our Cabernet Sauvignon from De Luz Vineyard. We are located in northern San Diego county, in De Luz Canyon, Fallbrook.

Scenic Valley Ranch Vineyards

27012 Scenic Valley Rd. Ramona CA 92065 619-884-3514
scenicvalleyranch@gmail.com http://www.scenicvalleyranch.com

Open: Sat. & Sun. 11 am–6 pm.

Amenities: Events, Tasting.

Varietals: Albarino, Cabernet Franc, Merlot, Petite Sirah.

Scenic Valley Ranch is a boutique winery located on the outskirts of Ramona in beautiful Ballena Valley. Here, we are crafting wine from grapes that are hand harvested from our estate as well as Ramona Valley vineyards.

Schwaesdall Winery

17677 Rancho De Oro Drive Ramona CA 92065 760-789-7542
shirley@schwaesdallwinery.com http://www.schwaesdallwinery.com

Open: Sat. & Sun. 11 am–6 pm (5 pm when daylight savings ends).

Amenities: Events, Music, Tasting.

Varietals: Cabernet Sauvignon, Chardonnay, Merlot, Port, Syrah, Zinfandel.

John Schwaesdall, a San Diego native, started making wine from some of the old vineyards in Ramona that were planted in 1950's. He has since planted 4 1/2 acres of various red and white wine grapes.

Shadow Mountain Vineyards

34680 Highway 79 Warner Springs CA 92086 760-782-0778
info@shadowmountainvineyards.com https://shadowmountainvineyards.com/

Open: Fri. thru Sun. 11am–5 pm.

Amenities: Music, Picnic, Tasting.

Varietals: Chardonnay, Merlot, Muscat Canelli, Sauvignon Blanc, Viognier.

Shadow Mountain Vineyards is the oldest producing vineyard in San Diego County, producing award-winning wines which beat vintages from the country's most famous wine regions.

Sierra Roble Winery & Vineyard

34810 Highway 79 Warner Springs CA 92086 760-892-2133
diana@loosenfarms.com https://www.sierraroble.com

Open: Fri. 12–5 pm, Sat. & Sun. 11 am–5 pm.

Amenities: Picnic, Tasting, Wine Club.

Varietals: Cabernet Franc, Cabernet Sauvignon, Rose, Sauvignon Blanc.

Our winery located in east San Diego County has a vast selection of ever changing and award winning wines. We invite you to come up for wine tasting while you enjoy the view on our outdoor patio. Pets and picnics welcome!

Sky Valley Cellars

16729 Sky Valley Dr. Ramona CA 92065 760-896-2685
info@skyvalleycellars.com https://www.skyvalleycellars.com

Open: Fri. 2–7 pm by appointment only, Sat. & Sun. 1–7 pm. Call for gate code.

Amenities: Tasting, Wine Club.

Varietals: Petite Sirah, Rose, Sangiovese, Syrah.

We are a family owned and operated vineyard & boutique winery nested in beautiful rolling hills of Ramona, a short drive from San Diego Coastal area.

Solterra Winery & Kitchen

934 North Coast Hwy 101 Leucadia CA 92024 760-230-2970
events@solterrawinery.com https://solterrawinery.com

Open: Thu. 3:30–9 pm, Fri. 3:30–10 pm, Sat. 12–10 pm, Sun. 12–8:30 pm.

Amenities: Events, Food, Tasting, Weddings, Wine Club.

Varietals: Cabernet Sauvignon, Chardonnay, Malbec, Merlot, Petit Verdot, Petite Sirah, Zinfandel.

Solterra is situated a couple of blocks from the beach in beautiful north county San Diego. Our goal is to offer an educational and satisfying wine experience to residents who will be able to enjoy the process and our wines locally.

Spanish Peacock Winery, Inc.

16987 Lyons Valley Road Jamul CA 91935 619-710-9108
https://spanishpeacockwinery.com/contact/

Open: Reservations only.

Amenities: Tasting.

Varietals: Cabernet Sauvignon, Mourvèdre, Pinot Noir, Rose, Syrah.

Spanish Peacock Winery is honored to host a private tasting for you and share the history and information that inspired the development of these wines. The wines attempt to add a new dimension to your wine list with vintages unique to Jamul, the San Diego wine industry, and an Old-world style of wines.

Speckle Rock Vineyards

16138 Highland Valley Road Escondido CA 92025 760-789-1287
info@srvwines.com https://www.specklerockvineyards.com/

Open: Thu. thru Sun. 1–7 pm.

Amenities: Food, Tasting, Wine Club.

Varietals: Chardonnay, Grenache, Merlot, Petite Sirah, Pinot Noir, Sangiovese, Sauvignon Blanc, Sparkling Wine, Tempranillo.

We named our wines 'Speckle Rock' as a symbol of endurance through tough times. Along with their symbolism, these rocks in their decomposed state are what contribute to our soil quality and give our wines a true expression of place.

Sunrise Vineyards

16620 Highland Valley Road Ramona CA 92065 858-334-9985
sunrisevineyards@gmail.com http://sunrisevineyardsandwinery.com

Open: Sat. & Sun. 12–7 pm.

Amenities: Events, Music, Tasting, Wine Club.

Varietals: Cabernet Sauvignon, Merlot, Sangiovese, Syrah.

We make all of the wines we sell, and all of our wines are made from grapes grown either onsite or in vineyards within 1.5 miles from the winery as the crow flies. At Sunrise Vineyards you get a wine that truly reflects the Ramona Valley American Viticultural Area.

Sunshine Mountain Vineyard

2286 Sunshine Mountain Road San Marcos CA 92069 760-798-3741
info@sunshinemountainwines.com https://www.sunshinemountainwines.com

Open: Thu. thru Sun. 12–7 pm.

Amenities: Events, Tasting, Weddings, Wine Club.

Varietals: Cabernet Franc, Cabernet Sauvignon, Chardonnay, Merlot, Riesling, Rose, Sauvignon Blanc, Viognier, Zinfandel.

Indulge in the breathtaking view and exceptional taste of Sunshine Mountain Vineyard. Situated on the hilltops of North San Diego, our vineyard boasts panoramic views of the city and its own unique soil that creates a perfect blend of California wilderness and European finesse.

Three Hills Winery

16805 Highland Valley Rd. Ramona CA 92065 619-507-7920
Info@ThreeHillsWinery.com https://www.threehillswinery.com

Open: Sat. & Sun. 11:30 am–4:30 pm.

Amenities: Events, Food, Music, Tasting, Wine Club.

Varietals: Cabernet Sauvignon, Merlot, Pinot Grigio, Port Syrah, Zinfandel.

The wines at Three Hills are produced in the Italian style and aged in lightly toasted French oak barrels from 18 to 30 months, depending on the wine. Their style aims to enhance the flavors of each grape varietal and not overpower the delicate aromas with the more heavily toasted oaks.

Toasted Oak Vineyards & Winery

190 Red Mountain Ln. Fallbrook CA 92028 760-420-3678
toastedoakwinery3@gmail.com https://www.toastedoakwinery.com

Open: Fri. thru Sun. 12–5 pm.

Amenities: Tasting.

Varietals: Cabernet Franc, Merlot, Syrah.

Toasted Oak Winery is a mom and pop operation that began in 2008, naming their future winery after the one surviving tree on the property, a "toasted" oak tree. Nine years later, after clearing, planting the vines, and building the winery, they were able to open their tasting room for business.

Trevi Hills Winery

13010 Muth Valley Rd. Lakeside CA 92040 619-443-0583
michael@trevihillswinery.com https://www.trevihillswinery.com

Open: Thu. thru Sun. 11 am–7 pm.

Amenities: Tasting, Wine Club.

Varietals: Pinot Noir, Sangiovese, Syrah.

Our nine year old vines consist of Sauvignon Blanc, Sparkling Wine, Syrah, Sangiovese and Primitivo. with the newest plantings of Merlot, Grenache, Mourvèdre, Malbec, Tempranillo and Montepulciano.

Triple B Ranches

15030 Vesper Road Valley Center CA 92082 760-749-1200
winery@triplebranches.com https://www.triplebranches.com/visiting

Open: Fri. thru Sat. 1–5 pm, Sun. 1–4 pm.

Amenities: Tasting.

Varietals: Cabernet Sauvignon, Chenin Blanc, Merlot, Syrah, Zinfandel.

Triple B Ranches is a family business dedicated to growing quality wine grapes and seasonal produce. We hope you'll raise a glass to the work, the craft and the tradition that brings only the best wine to the bottle.

Turtle Rock Ridge Vineyard Winery

18351 Woods Hill Lane Ramona CA 92065 760-789-5555
tasting@turtlerockridge.com http://turtlerockridge.com

Open: Thu. & Fri. 2–6 pm, Sat. & Sun. 12–6 pm.

Amenities: Tasting, Tours.

Varietals: Cabernet Franc, Cabernet Sauvignon, Chardonnay, Sangiovese, Sauvignon Blanc, Zinfandel.

Our wines are made from the very best grapes grown both in our vineyard and sourced locally within the Ramona and California wine region. We feature a selection of red and white wines, We are very proud to share the fact that many of our wines have won awards.

Valentina Vineyards

17035 Campo Road Dulzura CA 91917 858-245-2824
lance@valentinavineyards.com https://valentinavineyards.com

Open: Sat. & Sun. 11 am–5 pm. Reservations only for Mon. thru Fri.

Amenities: Tasting.

Varietals: Chardonnay, Sauvignon Blanc.

We are a family owned vineyard supplying the San Diego market with the best wine grapes and wine. We use natural and sustainable growing methods and have over 20 varieties of wine grapes for the wine that you are seeking.

VecchieOso Vineyard

19365 Elena Lane Jamul CA 91935 619-922-0002
info@vecchieosovineyard.com https://vecchieosovineyard.com/

Open: Opening Sep. 16, 2023. Sat. & Sun. 11 am–6 pm. Reservations needed from Mon. thru Fri.

Amenities: Events, Tasting, Wine Club.

Varietals: Barbera, Cabernet Sauvignon, Montepulciano, Nebbiolo, Pinot Gris, Syrah.

We feel our vineyard is more than a patch of land with grapevines; it's a living testament to the power of creativity, passion, and the love we share. It has become a symbol of the beauty that emerges when one combines hard work with a genuine love for what they do.

Vina Ramona Wines

657 E. Old Julian Highway Ramona CA 92065 760-315-8068
info@vinaramona.com https://vinaramona.com

Open: Sat. & Sun. 1–5 pm.

Amenities: Food, Music, Tasting.

Varietals: Cabernet Sauvignon, Chardonnay, Merlot, Petite Sirah, Sangiovese, Syrah, Tempranillo, Zinfandel and a Lushee.

Don't let the open trailer fool you, it is their tasting room. Their tasting pours are generous and they are super friendly wine servers. Vina Ramona is a must stop on your winery tour of Ramona.

Vineyard 1924, The

1924 E. Mission Road Fallbrook CA 92028 760-651-2182
TheVineyard1924@gmail.com http://thevineyard1924.com/

Open: Fri. thru Sat. 3–8 pm, Sun. 11 am–6 pm. Group reservations only.

Amenities: Events, Tasting, Weddings.

Varietals: Cabernet Sauvignon, Sauvignon Blanc.

The Vineyard 1924 is centrally located in the rolling hills of Fallbrook; the property showcases summit views of Mount San Jacinto, sweeping images of the valley, and dramatic sunsets.

Vineyard Grant James

25260 Old Julian Hwy. Ramona CA 92065 760-206-3481
info@vineyardgrantjames.com http://www.vineyardgrantjames.com

Open: Fri. thru Sun. 12–6 pm.

Amenities: Events, Food, Tasting, Wine Club.

Varietals: Chardonnay, Malbec, Nebbiolo, Sangiovese, Sauvignon Blanc, Syrah, Viognier, Zinfandel.

In the Spring of 2009, the first three acres were planted at Vineyard Grant James, and now there are seven and a half acres planted on our beautiful property. Our main varietals include Syrah, Merlot, Sangiovese, Orange Muscat, Greco, Refosco and Nebbiolo.

Volcan Mountain Winery

1255 Julian Orchards Drive Julian CA 92036 760-765-3267
Melanie.vmw@gmail.com https://www.facebook.com/volcanmountainwinery/

Open: Fri. thru Mon. 11 am–5 pm.

Amenities: Events, Tasting, Wine Club.

Varietals: Barbera, Cabernet Franc, Cabernet Sauvignon, Chardonnay, , Malbec, Rose, Sangiovese, Syrah, Zinfandel.

Volcan Mountain Winery (formerly J. Jenkin Winery), established in 2015, is nestled at the base of the picturesque Volcan Mountain. Their tasting room, winery, vineyard, and orchard are only a mere 2-mile scenic drive from the historic town center of Julian with a newly remodeled tasting room.

Walnut Tree Ranch

25303 Mesa Grande Road Santa Ysabel CA 92070
https://walnuttreeranch.com/

Open: Thu. thru Sun. 1–3 pm. Reservations only.

Amenities: Tasting.

Varietals: Cabernet Sauvignon, Sangiovese, Zinfandel.

We are a small boutique winery in San Diego County's picturesque backcountry. Our vineyard includes the red varieties Sangiovese, Zinfandel and Cabernet Sauvignon.

Westfall Winery

1910 Buckman Springs Road Campo CA 91906 619-454-1711
https://www.westfallvineyards.com/

Open: Reservations only.

Amenities: Tasting.

Varietals: Grenache, Mourvèdre, Orange Muscat, Sangiovese, Primitivo, Sauvignon Blanc, Syrah, Zinfandel.

For years Richard Westfall has been building a reputation for crafting stunning wines from fruit produced on his Estate vineyards in San Diego's East County. His new Westfall Winery is now open and an initial selection of current vintages is available to the public for tasting and purchase.

Witch Creek Winery

2906 Carlsbad Blvd. Carlsbad CA 92008 760-720-7499
events@witchcreekwinery.com https://www.witchcreekwinery.com

Open: Wed. 12–7 pm, Thu. 12–8 pm, Fri. 12–9 pm, Sat. 12–10 pm, Sun. 12–7 pm.

Amenities: Events, Tasting, Wine Club.

Varietals: Cabernet Franc, Cabernet Sauvignon, Merlot, Petite Sirah.

Witch Creek Winery is San Diego's oldest Urban Winery originally founded in 1993 and relocated to Carlsbad in 1996. We specialize in making easy drinking, consumer friendly wines.

Woof'n Rose Winery

17073 Garjan Lane Ramona CA 92065 760-788-4818 Marilyn@Woofnrose.com
http://woofnrose.com

Open: Sat. & Sun. 12–5 pm.

Amenities: Tasting.

Varietals: Albariño, Barbera, Cabernet Franc, Cabernet Sauvignon, Merlot, Petite Sirah plus many Blends.

Woof'n Rose makes all of its wines from Ramona Valley grapes. Their specialty is Cabernet Franc and includes all of the other classic Bordeaux varietals, Cabernet Sauvignon, Merlot, Malbec, and Petit Verdot, including Carmenere, as well as Grenache Noir, Alicante Bouschet, and Montepulciano.

ZXQ Vineyards

15454 Highlands Crest Way Escondido CA 92025 619-736-3230
info@zxqvineyards.com https://www.zxqvineyards.com/

Open: Fri. 2–7 pm, Sat. & Sun. 12–7 pm (last call at 6 pm).

Amenities: Music, Tasting, Wine Club.

Varietals: Cabernet Franc, Cabernet Sauvignon, Merlot, Rose, Zinfandel.

The vineyard is planted with producing vines of Zinfandel, Cabernet Sauvignon, Cabernet Franc, and Petite Sirah. Our first bottling was the 2015 vintage. Petite Sirah was planted in 2017 and was first harvested in 2019. Bottling of the Petite Sirah occurred 2021.

Riverside County Wine Region

Temecula Valley AVA

With more than 50 wineries to choose from, the Temecula Valley AVA is the largest designated wine region in the South Coast wine region of California and it's where more than 90% of the wineries are located in Riverside County. The name Temecula is reportedly a local Native American term for 'the land of sunshine and mist,' and whether faithful or not, this translation accurately describes the climate in the Temecula Valley.

As the valley heats up during the morning, warm air rises upwards and further inland, creating a pressure differential. Natural convection draws cool Pacific Ocean air into the valley through gaps in the Santa Ana Mountains (the coastal ranges which separate Orange County from Riverside County).

These 'Santa Ana winds' can become quite strong, and in 2007 blew a minor scrub fire up into a major wildfire which scorched much of the Temecula Valley area. A similar climatic effect blows through the Chino Hills 50 miles (80km) to the north, cooling the Cucamonga Valley AVA.

Temecula lies 22 miles (35km) east of the Pacific coast, so the valley enjoys a relatively strong maritime influence. As cool, moist air rolls up the valley, it condenses to form mist and refreshes the local vineyards, preparing them for the hot southern California afternoon. This mist is lighter than the fog found in the lower-lying terroirs of Napa and Sonoma, and reflects sunshine rather than deflecting it.

Were the Santa Anas slightly higher or the valley slightly further from the coast, Temecula would be significantly hotter and drier than it is, making quality viticulture more of a challenge. Very few places on Temecula's latitude (33 degrees north) support quality viticulture: Lebanon and Israel are the only remotely obvious examples.

However, the Temecula Valley terroir is well suited to grape growing, with free-draining, granite soils supporting the vines. The higher elevation sees most vineyards planted at 1,500 feet (457m) above sea level, which contributes to cooler nights to allow for acid retention in the grapes. Irrigation is necessary in this very dry region, allowing growers to control yields and grape quality.

Almost half of all vines in the Temecula Valley were destroyed by Pierce's Disease in the 1990s, but ultimately this seems to have worked in the region's favor. Not only are more disease-resistant varieties being planted, but a new range of quality wines has emerged. In the past, the region was mostly known for its value-for-money, delicate, low-alcohol white wines. Post-Pierce's Disease plantings focus firmly on the more lucrative, big Mediterranean reds.

Temecula Valley Tempranillo wines are notable for their complex aromas of plums and berries. Sangiovese wines from the AVA boast fat, ripe tannins and flavors decidedly riper than their Italian counterparts. Syrah has recently won the region many accolades for its round, fleshy style and generous, full flavors. Cabernet Franc has emerged as the star of the Bordeaux varieties and is fast earning a reputation for producing elegant, aromatic styles full of complex flavors.

History From Humble Beginnings

In 1967 Vincenzo and Audrey Cilurzo purchased 40 acres of property down a long dirt road known as Long Valley Road (soon to become Rancho California Road). The Cilurzo's established the first modern commercial vineyard in the Temecula Valley in 1968.

In 1974, the founding of Callaway Winery (by Ely Callaway, of golf fame) marked the beginning of large production winemaking in the Temecula Valley. Callaway, sold the winery in 1981 to Hiram Walker and Sons.

John Poole opened Mount Palomar Winery in 1975, and in 1978 the Cilurzos opened another Temecula winery at a new site. Their original vineyard, Temecula's oldest, is now owned by Maurice Carrie Winery.

Though Temecula became an incorporated city in 1989, the region officially became an American Viticultural Area (AVA) in 1984. Modern Temecula Wine Country is located east of the Rainbow Gap in Riverside County and the Temecula wine community has grown considerably since its humble beginnings.

Riverside County Wineries A to Z

Akash Winery

39730 Calle Contento Temecula CA 92591 info@akashwinery.com
https://www.akashwinery.com

Open: Mon., Wed. & Thu. 12–6 pm, Tue. 12–8 pm, Fri.& Sun. 11 am–6 pm, Sat. 11 am–8 pm.

Amenities: Events, Food, Music, Tasting, Tours, Wine Club.

Varietals: Cabernet Franc, Cabernet Sauvignon, Malbec, Petite Sirah, Pinot Noir, Rose, Sauvignon Blanc, Zinfandel.

Visit our gorgeous, open-air patio, where you'll find far more than beautiful views and amazing wine. We're loved by locals and out-of-towners alike, thanks to the happy energy and friendly faces of our knowledgeable team.

Altisima Winery

37440 De Portola Road Temecula CA 92592 951-422-2525
wineclub@altisimawinery.com https://altisimawinery.com

Open: Mon. thru Thu. 11 am–5 pm, Fri. thru Sun. 11 am–6 pm.

Amenities: Events, Food, Tasting, Tours, Weddings, Wine Club.

Varietals: Cabernet Sauvignon, Port, Sparkling Wine, Zinfandel.

At Altisima Winery, we celebrate the history and heritage of one of California's oldest wine regions, by paying homage to the Spanish captain who memorialized the region. Join us in celebrating our Spanish roots with a world-class modern touch. We look forward to exploring with you!

Baily Vineyard & Winery

33440 La Serena Way Temecula CA 92591 951-676-9463
https://bailywinery.com

Open: Sun. thru Fri. 11 am–5 pm, Sat. 10 am–5 pm.

Amenities: Events, Food, Tasting, Wine Club.

Varietals: Cabernet Franc, Cabernet Sauvignon, Malbec, Merlot, Port, Sauvignon Blanc, Sémillon.

Exciting News! Baily Vineyard & Winery has been named one of the 25 best wineries in the United States in an article by Katy Spratte Joyce in Reader's Digest magazine, and one of the 15 best wineries in the US by TripsToDiscover.com.

Bel Vino Winery

33515 Rancho California Road Temecula CA 92591 951-676-6414 info@BelVinoWinery.com https://www.belvinowinery.com

Open: Wed. thru Mon. 11 am–5 pm.

Amenities: Food, Music, Private Events, Tasting, Tours, Weddings, Wine Club.

Varietals: Cabernet Franc, Cabernet Sauvignon, Chardonnay, Malbec, Merlot, Muscat, Petite Sirah, Pinot Noir, Riesling, Rose, Sauvignon Blanc, Sparkling Wine, Syrah, Viognier, Zinfandel.

The Winery has a rustic authenticity, and its Barrel Tasting Room is warm, friendly and educational. Under visionary new ownership since late 2011, the Winery offers a portfolio of 30 to 40 great wines, including highly rated gold medal winners and Southern California's best red wines.

Bella Vista Winery

41220 Calle Contento Temecula CA 92592 951-676-5250 bellavistawinery@aol.com https://www.bellavistawinery.com

Open: Mon. thru Sun. 12–5 pm.

Amenities: Events, Tasting, Wine Club.

Varietals: Cabernet Franc, Cabernet Sauvignon, Chardonnay, Malbec, Merlot, Muscat Canelli, Petite Sirah, Rose, Sangiovese, Sauvignon Blanc, Sparkling Wine, Syrah, Tempranillo, Viognier.

Vines were planted on our Calle Contento property in 1968 by the first owner and still producing adjacent to the winery, which was built in 1978. Imre and his wife Gizella Cziraki purchased the former Cilurzo Winery what is now known as Bella Vista Winery, the location of Temecula's first commercial vineyard.

Big Nose Winery

42100 Main St. Temecula CA 92590 951-515-3229 BigNoseWinery@gmail.com https://www.bignosefamilywinery.com/tasting-room

Open: Thu. 12–6 pm, Fri. & Sat. 12–8 pm, Sun. 11 am–6 pm.

Amenities: Tasting, Wine Club.

Varietals: Cabernet Franc, Merlot, Petite Sirah, Pinot Grigio, Rose, Sangiovese, Sauvignon Blanc, Zinfandel.

Big Nose Winery is a locally owned family winery dedicated to the art of winemaking and providing a delightful grape-to-glass experience. Our wines are produced from the best variety of grapes possible–free from defects, well-balanced, and flavorful.

BOTTAIA Winery

35601 Rancho California Road Temecula CA 92591 951-365-3388
frontdesk@bottaiawinery.com https://www.bottaiawinery.com

Open: Wed. thru Sun. 11 am–6 pm.

Amenities: Events, Food, Music, Pool, Tasting, Wine Club.

Varietals: Barbera, Montepulciano, Pinot Grigio, Rose, Sangiovese, plus large variety of sweet Italian late harvest and dessert wines.

BOTTAIA Winery is designed to enhance your wine country experience without the crowds and operates by reservation. Seating is limited, and advance reservations are highly recommended for all experiences.

Briar Rose Winery

41720 Calle Cabrillo Temecula CA 92592 951-308-1098
Katie@BriarRoseWinery.com https://www.briarrosewinery.com/welcome.html

Open: Fri. thru Sun. 12–5 pm. Reservations only.

Amenities: Picnic, Tasting, Weddings, Wine Club.

Varietals: Barbera, Cabernet Sauvignon, Muscat Canelli, Pinot Noir, Rose, Syrah, Tempranillo, Viognier.

Briar Rose Winery has the proud distinction of being Temecula Valley's premier boutique winery. We are family owned and family operated. Our winery produces handcrafted, small lot, premium, artisan wines made from the most intensely flavored grapes from our lush vineyards.

Callaway Vineyard & Winery

32720 Rancho California Road Temecula CA 92591 951-676-4001
marketing@callawaywinery.com https://www.callawaywinery.com

Open: Mon. thru Sun. 11 am–6 pm.

Amenities: Events, Tasting, Tours, Weddings, Wine Club.

Varietals: Cabernet Sauvignon, Chardonnay, Muscat Canelli, Nebbiolo, Petit Verdot, Petite Sirah, Pinot Gris, Rose, Roussanne, Sangiovese, Sauvignon Blanc, Syrah, Viognier, Zinfandel.

Founded in 1974, Callaway was the first winery to open its doors in the Temecula Valley. Approachable, flavorful and extremely well-balanced wines are synonymous with the Callaway name. We invite you taste our wines at our Temecula Winery.

Canyon Crest Winery

301 E. Alessandro Blvd. Suite #3A Riverside CA 92508 951-369-9463
canyoncrestwineryriverside@gmail.com
https://www.thecanyoncrestwinery.com/

Open: Tue. thru Thu. 4–9 pm, Fri. 4–10 pm, Sat. 3–10 pm, Sun. 12–4 pm.

Amenities: Events, Tasting, Urban Winery/Wine Bar, Wine Club.

Varietals: Cabernet Sauvignon, Chardonnay, Malbec, Merlot, Pinot Noir, Port, Rose, Sangiovese, Sauvignon Blanc, Sangria, Zinfandel.

Canyon Crest Winery brings a unique and boutique winery concept right in the city limits of Riverside. Canyon Crest Winery produces wines from around the world at our rustic Canyon Crest Towne Centre location.

Canopy Wine Lounge

175 N. Palm Canyon Dr. Palm Springs CA 92262 760-656-0054
info@canopywinelounge.com https://www.canopywinelounge.com/about

Open: Thu. thru Sat. 4–10 pm, Sun. & Mon. 4–9 pm. Reservations only.

Amenities: Events, Food, Tasting, Urban Winery/Wine Bar.

Varietals: Cabernet Franc, Cabernet Sauvignon, Chardonnay, Grenache, Merlot, Pinot Noir, Riesling, Sauvignon Blanc, Shiraz, Sparkling.

Welcome to Canopy Wine Lounge, a standout destination nestled in the vibrant landscape of Palm Springs. This unique lounge blends the elevated elegance of a curated wine cellar with the inviting charm of a neighborhood favorite.

Carter Estate Winery & Resort

34450 Rancho California Road Temecula CA 92591 951-587-9463
https://www.carterestatewinery.com

Open: Mon. thru Fri. 12–5 pm, Sat. & Sun. 11 am–6 pm.

Amenities: Food, Lodging, Tasting, Weddings, Wine Club.

Varietals: Cabernet Sauvignon, Chardonnay, Malbec, Merlot, Sangiovese, Sparkling Wine, Syrah, Viognier.

Surrounded by 112 acres of carefully tended vines, Carter Estate Winery elevates the Southern California winery experience to Napa levels and beyond. What makes our grapes so special is the combination of the rich soil and generous sunshine.

Chapin Family Vineyards

36084 Summitville Street Temecula CA 92592 951-506-2935
wineclub@chapinfamilyvineyards.com
https://www.chapinfamilyvineyards.com

Open: Sun. thru Thu. 10 am–5 pm, Fri. & Sat. 10 am–6 pm.

Amenities: Events, Food, Tasting, Tours, Weddings, Wine Club.

Varietals: Albarino, Cabernet Franc, Cabernet Sauvignon, Chardonnay, Montepulciano, Muscat, Petit Verdot, Petite Sirah, Rose, Sauvignon Blanc, Sparkling Wine, Syrah, Viognier.

At Chapin Family Vineyards we hold our protocols to the highest of standards. From vineyard to table, nothing is overlooked. We invite you to take a small vacation and visit our boutique winery and relax with us on the veranda overlooking our beautiful vineyards.

Churon Winery

33233 Rancho California Road Temecula CA 92591 951-694-9070
wineclub@innatchuronwinery.com https://innatchuronwinery.com

Open: Mon. thru Thu. 11 am–5 pm, Fri. & Sat. 10 am–6 pm, Sun. 10 am–5 pm.

Amenities: Food, Lodging, Music, Tasting, Tours, Weddings, Wine Club.

Varietals: Barbera, Chardonnay, Moscato, Pinot Grigio, Port, Rose, Sauvignon Blanc, Sparkling Wine, Syrah, Viognier, Zinfandel.

Indulge in the exquisite world of Churon wines, crafted by the renowned winemaker, Tim Kramer. With a wealth of winemaking expertise, Tim has masterfully created a collection of Award-Winning estate wines that embody the essence of Churon.

Cougar Vineyard & Winery

39870 De Portola Rd. Temecula CA 92592 951-491-0825
info@cougarvineyards.com https://cougarwinery.com

Open: Mon. thru Sun. 11 am–6 pm. Reservations only.

Amenities: Events, Food, Tasting, Wine Club.

Varietals: Barbera, Nebbiolo, Pinot Grigio, Port, Sangiovese, Sangria, Sauvignon Blanc, Sparkling Wine and Italian varietals.

In 2005 we planted Sangiovese, Aglianico, Montepulciano, and Vermentino since then we've added Falanghina, Ciliegiolo, Prosecco and Piedirosso. Next door we've planted Primitivo, Arneis, Malvasia Bianca, Pinot Grigio, Sagrantino, Piedirosso and Lambrusca di Alessandria.

Danza Del Sol Winery

39050 De Portola Rd. Temecula CA 92592 951-302-6363
a.zdunek@danzadelsolwinery.com https://www.danzadelsolwinery.com

Open: Mon. thru Sun. 11 am–6 pm.

Amenities: Events, Music, Tasting, Tours, Weddings, Wine Club.

Varietals: Gewürztraminer, Grenache, Pinot, Rose, Sangiovese, Tempranillo.

Nestled in a 40-acre vineyard, Danza del Sol Winery is located on the De Portola Wine Trail in the heart of Temecula Valley, just 45 minutes from San Diego. Our winery reflects the spirit of "The Valley" rustic, authentic and bold.

Doffo Winery

36083 Summitville St. Temecula CA 92592 951-676-6989 info@doffowines.com
https://doffowines.com

Open: Sun. thru Thu. 11 am–5 pm, Fri. & Sat. 11 am–6 pm.

Amenities: Music, Tasting, Tours, Weddings, Wine Club.

Varietals: Cabernet Sauvignon, Malbec, Petite Sirah, Port, Rose, Sparkling Wine, Syrah, Zinfandel and Italian varietals.

Founded by Marcelo Doffo in 1997, this family owned and operated winery produces many award-winning wines and has earned a stellar reputation in the region for its Malbec, Zinfandel, Cabernet Sauvignon, Syrah, and its unique red blends.

Europa Village

41150 Via Europa Temecula CA 92591 951-506-1818 info@europavillage.com https://www.europavillage.com/visit-us/

Open: Three tasting rooms:

Bolero Tasting Room open Mon. thru Sun. 11 am–6 pm with extended hours from 11 am–8 pm on Tue., Thu. & Sat.

C'est La Vie Tasting Room open Mon. thru Thu. 1–5 pm, Sat. & Sun. 10 am–5 pm with extended hours from 10 am–8 pm on Fri.

Vienza Tasting Room open Mon. 12–7 pm, Tue. thru Thu. 12–6 pm, Fri. thru Sun. 11 am–7 pm.

Amenities: Events, Food, Lodging, Tasting, Weddings, Wine Club.

Varietals: Cabernet Sauvignon, Malbec, Merlot, Muscat Canelli, Pinot Noir, Sparkling Wine, Syrah.

Discover something new through the lens of something old. At Europa Village we invite you to unearth a different kind of winery experience—three charming destinations set in the old-world villages of Spain (Bolero), France (C'est La Vie), and Italy (Vienza) that all come together as one grand resort.

Falkner Winery

40620 Calle Contento Temecula CA 92591 951-676-8231 info@falknerwinery.com https://falknerwinery.com

Open: Mon. thru Sun. 10 am–5 pm.

Amenities: Food, Tasting, Tours, Weddings, Wine Club.

Varietals: Cabernet Sauvignon, Chardonnay, Merlot, Port, Riesling, Rose, Sauvignon Blanc, Syrah, Viognier.

Escape into a world of elegance and experience a haven where memories begin. Falkner Winery is a long time in the making and our story is one of passion, perseverance and of course great wine.

Fazeli Cellars Winery

37320 De Portola Road Temecula CA 92592 951-303-3366
https://fazelicellars.com

Open: Mon. thru Sun. 11 am–6 pm.

Amenities: Events, Food, Tasting, Tours, Weddings, Wine Club.

Varietals: Cabernet Sauvignon, Meritage, Montepulciano, Rose, Shiraz, and many Persian varietals.

Nestled in the picturesque rolling hills of the De Portola Wine Trail, Fazeli Cellars soars as a state-of-the-art winery offering a combination of stunning architecture, breathtaking scenic beauty, and the finest selection of boutique wines the region has to offer.

Foot Path Winery

36650 Glen Oaks Rd. Temecula CA 92592 951-265-9951
info@FootPathWinery.com https://footpathwinery.com

Open: Mon. thru Fri. 12–5 pm, Sat. & Sun. 10 am–5 pm.

Amenities: Tasting, Wine Club.

Varietals: Barbera, Cabernet Franc, Malbec, Merlot, Mourvèdre, Petite Sirah, Sangiovese, Syrah, Zinfandel.

We use old world techniques of wine creation, while taking delicate care of our wines through every step of the crafting process. Foot Path Winery is the only certified users of organic grapes in all of the Temecula Valley area.

Frangipani Estate Winery

39750 De Portola Road Temecula CA 92592 951-699-8845
frangipaniwine@aol.com https://frangipaniwinery.com

Open: Mon. thru Sun. 10 am–5 pm (most days).

Amenities: Tasting, Wine Club.

Varietals: Cabernet Franc, Cabernet Sauvignon, Grenache, Muscat Canelli, Rose, Sauvignon Blanc, Syrah, Tempranillo.

Frangipani Estate Winery overlooks its vineyards along the De Portola Wine Trail. Guests are treated with breathtaking views of the estate and experience a unique wine tasting patio service like no other by allowing guest to stay seated and relax all while being served Reserve Style wine.

Gershon Bachus Vintners

37750 De Portola Road Temecula CA 92592 877-458-8428
info@gershonbachus.com https://www.gershonbachus.com

Open: Mon. thru Thu. 12–6 pm, Fri. thru Sun. 11 am–6 pm.

Amenities: Events, Music, Tasting, Weddings.

Varietals: Cabernet Franc, Cabernet Sauvignon, Grenache, Merlot, Mourvèdre, Sangiovese, Syrah, Tempranillo, Zinfandel.

We produce wines that we love to share. Currently, we offer 12 reds and 3 whites that will meet even the most discerning of palettes. With each new wine, we look to maximize the varietal's natural flavor and beautiful bouquet.

Halter Ranch Vineyard Estate

41300 Ave. Biona Temecula CA 92591 805-226-9455 visit@halterranch.com
https://www.halterranch.com/visit

Open: Mon. thru Sun. 10:30 am–5 pm.

Amenities: Tasting, Wine Club.

Varietals:, Cabernet Sauvignon, Carignan, Grenache, Malbec, Petit Verdot, Rose, Sparkling Wine, Syrah, Tannat, Tempranillo.

Charming and relaxed, our Tasting Room offers an escape from pretense. Enjoy the energetic, inviting, and enchanting feel of Temecula Wine Country paired with the award-winning wines of the Halter Ranch portfolio (formerly Hart Winery).

hyphen- Wine Shop

1007 N. Palm Canyon Dr. Palm Springs CA 92262 760-459-9199
info@hyphenpsp.com https://www.hyphenpsp.com/

Open: Mon. thru Sat. 10 am–7 pm, Sun. 11 am–5 pm.

Amenities: Events, Tasting, Tours, Urban Winery/Wine Bar.

Varietals: Albarino, Barbera, Bordeaux, Cabernet Franc, Cabernet Sauvignon, Chardonnay, Chenin Blanc, Grenache, Malbec, Montepulciano, Pinot Grigio, Pinot Noir, Riesling, Rose, Sparkling, Syrah, Tempranillo, Viognier.

We're a Palm Springs wine store dedicated to connecting our customers to delicious, high-quality natural wines. But it goes much deeper than that. Hyphens are connectors. And we're no exception.

Julie's Dream Winery

39820 Calle Contento Temecula CA 92591 951-271-6329
karrie@juliesdreamwinery.com https://www.juliesdreamwinery.com

Open: Mon. thru Sun. 12–5:30 pm.

Amenities: Music, Tasting, Weddings.

Varietals: Cabernet Sauvignon, Chardonnay, Petite Sirah, Sauvignon Blanc.

The perfect getaway situated on 25 acres of estate vineyards surrounded by the Temecula Valley Wine Country. A place where you can visit, enjoy, and take part in a memorable experience.

La Fata Cellars

41955 5th Street Temecula CA 92590 800-876-1657 support@lafatacellars.com
https://www.lafatacellars.com/

Open: Sun. thru Wed. 11 am–7 pm, Thu. thru Sat. 11 am–9 pm.

Amenities: Events, Music, Tasting, Wine Club.

Varietals: Cabernet Sauvignon, Chardonnay, Merlot, Petite Sirah, Pinot Noir, Sauvignon Blanc, Syrah, Viognier.

La Fata Cellars is more than a winery; it's a testament to tenacity, discipline, and an entrepreneurial drive that refused to be stifled. Their dreams of creating exquisite wines and building a family legacy became a reality when they planted their vineyard in Temecula Valley Wine Country in 2017.

Leonesse Cellars

38311 De Portola Road Temecula CA 92592 951-302-7601
https://www.leonesscellars.com

Open: Mon. thru Thu. 11:30 am–5 pm, Fri. 11:30 am–6 pm, Sat. 11 am–6 pm, Sun. 11 am–5 pm.

Amenities: Events, Food, Tasting, Tours, Weddings.

Varietals: Cabernet Franc, Cabernet Sauvignon, Grenache, Mourvèdre, Muscat Canelli, Rose, Sauvignon Blanc, Syrah, Viognier, Zinfandel.

Enjoy picturesque vineyard views while sampling our range of wines highlighting the very best of what Temecula has to offer. We have farmed the local community since the 1970s and are committed to producing wine from the highest quality local fruit.

Longshadow Ranch Winery

39847 Calle Contento Temecula CA 92591 951-587-6221
reservelongshadow@gmail.com https://www.longshadowranchwinery.com

Open: Mon. thru Fri. 12–5 pm, Sat. 12–8:30 pm, Sun. 11 am–5 pm.

Amenities: Events, Food, Tasting, Weddings, Wine Club.

Varietals: Cabernet Sauvignon, Malbec, Merlot, Sangiovese, Syrah, Tempranillo.

Bottled with pride, these wines are a reflection of our heritage. We hope you enjoy them as much as we have loved bringing them to you, and we invite you to come out and visit us here at the ranch.

Lorenzi Estate

36095 Monte De Oro Road Temecula CA 92592 951-506-1300
Lorenziestatewines@gmail.com https://lorenziestatewines.com/home-3

Open: Mon. thru Sun. 11 am–5 pm.

Amenities: Tasting, Wine Club.

Varietals: Cabernet Franc, Chardonnay, Grenache, Merlot, Petite Sirah, Pinot Noir, Syrah, Zinfandel.

California South Coast Wineries Guide

Grapes from legendary vineyards formed the genesis of the Lorenzi private label. From there, we set out to build one of Southern California's premium wineries.

Lorimar Vineyards

39990 Anza Road Temecula CA 92591 951-694-6699
wineclub@lorimarwinery.com https://www.lorimarwinery.com

Open: Sun. thru Thu. 11 am–5 pm, Fri. & Sat. 11 am–9 pm.

Amenities: Food, Music, Tasting, Tours, Weddings, Wine Club.

Varietals: Cabernet Franc, Cabernet Sauvignon, Chardonnay, Malbec, Merlot, Muscat Canelli, Petite Sirah, Rose, Sangiovese, Syrah, Viognier.

At Lorimar Vineyards and Winery we engage your senses with a blend of handcrafted and award-winning wine wines, live music, local art, gourmet food, and captivating views of the Temecula Valley. Lorimar wines are fruit forward and showcase dedication to producing the best product from grape to glass.

Lumier Winery

39555 Calle Contento Temecula CA 92591 951-972-0585
https://lumierewinery.com

Open: Fri. thru Sun. 11 am–6 pm.

Amenities: Tasting.

Varietals: Cabernet Franc, Cabernet Sauvignon, Merlot, Sauvignon Blanc.

Planted in 1980, the old vines were originally Sauvignon Blanc of which six acres still are. In 1987, the Kleiner family purchased the 21 acre vineyard property and began their life of growing grapes.

Masia de la Vinya

40230 De Portola Road Temecula CA 92592 951-303-3860
p.obrien@masiadelavinya.com https://www.masiadelavinya.com

Open: Thu. thru Mon. 11 am–6 pm.

Amenities: Events, Music, Tasting, Tours, Wine Club.

Varietals: Cabernet Sauvignon, Chardonnay, Malbec, Syrah.

Our boutique winery was thoughtfully designed to offer a casual, relaxed wine tasting experience with a scenic view of our vineyard, the mountains and the valley. Our philosophy is to offer handcrafted, unique wines which are fruit-forward and made to pair well with food.

Matin Du Bois Vintners

27495 Diaz Road Temecula CA 92590 951-387-4809
customercare@matindubois.com https://matindubois.com/

Open: Thu. thru Mon. 11 am–9 pm.

Amenities: Food, Tasting.

Varietals: Cabernet Franc, Pinot Grigio.

Matin Du Bois Vintners is a family-owned winery located in the Temecula Valley that was born out of an appreciation for the craftsmanship, tradition, and perfection of creating a great wine. As second-generation vintners, we strive to keep tradition a central part of winemaking.

Middle Ridge Winery

54301 N. Circle Drive Idyllwild CA 92549 951-659-9000
winetalk@middleridge.com https://www.middleridge.com/

Open: Fri. & Sat. 12–7 pm, Sun. & Mon. 12–6 pm.

Amenities: Events, Tasting, Wine Club.

Varietals: Cabernet Franc, Cabernet Sauvignon, Malbec, Meritage, Merlot, Muscat Canelli, Petite Sirah, Pinot Gris, Sparkling Wine, Syrah, Tempranillo.

Middle Ridge is a boutique winery headquartered in the mountain arts community of Idyllwild. The friendliness of the small town inspired winemaker Chris Johnston to bring people together with handcrafted, artisan wines in intimate settings.

Miramonte Winery

33410 Rancho California Rd. Temecula CA 92591 951-506-5500
hello@miramontewinery.com https://www.miramontewinery.com

Open: Thu. 11 am–6 pm, Sat. 11 am–8 pm, Sun. 11 am–7 pm.

Amenities: Events, Food, Tasting, Wine Club.

Varietals: Albarino, Cabernet Sauvignon, Moscato, Pinot Gris, Riesling, Rose, Sangria, Syrah, Tempranillo.

Founded in 2001 by Cane Vanderhoof, Miramonte has emerged as one of the most respected and forward thinking boutique wineries of southern California. Located in the heart of Temecula Valley, we are passionate about the traditional grapes varieties of southern France, Spain and Portugal.

Monte de Oro Winery

35820 Rancho California Rd. Temecula CA 92591 951-491-6551
kenzig@montedeoro.com https://montedeoro.com/

Open: Mon. & Tue. 12–5 pm, Wed. thru & Sun. 11 am–5 pm.

Amenities: Food, Tasting, Weddings, Wine Club.

Varietals: Cabernet Sauvignon, Merlot, Petite Sirah, Pinot Gris, Syrah, Tempranillo, Viognier, Zinfandel.

Monte De Oro's wines are crafted in a style to showcase the true varietal character of each grape variety, balanced with the fruit-forward territory of Temecula Valley and subtle influences from extended barrel aging in French, European and American oak barrels.

Mount Palomar Winery

33820 Rancho California Rd. Temecula CA 92591 951-676-5047
info@mountpalomar.com https://www.mountpalomarwinery.com

Open: Mon. thru Sun. 11 am–5 pm (hours subject to change).

Amenities: Events, Food, Music, Picnic, Tasting, Weddings, Wine Club.

Varietals: Cabernet Franc, Chardonnay, Port, Riesling, Rose, Sangiovese, Sauvignon Blanc, Sherry, Viognier.

The statement "Winemaking begins in the vineyard," is a cliche to some, but a guiding principle at Mount Palomar. Our estate vineyards are held to a high standard. We believe that wines should reflect a sense of harmony, presenting the taster with an array of sensations that are pleasing, yet complex.

Oak Mountain Winery

36522 Vía Verde Temecula CA 92592 951-699-9102
amanning@oakmountainwinery.com https://oakmountainwinery.com

Open: Mon. thru Sun. 11 am–5 pm.

Amenities: Cave, Events, Food, Tasting, Tours, Weddings, Wine Club.

Varietals: Cabernet Franc, Cabernet Sauvignon, Malbec, Merlot, Montepulciano, Mourvèdre, Petite Sirah, Rose, Sangiovese, Sauvignon Blanc, Sparkling Wine, Tempranillo.

Home to Southern California's only mined wine caves, Oak Mountain offers tours and tastings with our friendly and knowledgeable staff. We are known for our famous raspberry and strawberry champagnes and offer over 30 award winning wines.

Off the Rails Winery

41740 Enterprise Circle N. #109 (inside Black Market Brewing Company) Temecula CA 92593 951-458-6992 reservations@offtherailwinery.com https://www.offtherailswinery.com/

Open: Reservations only.

Amenities: Food, Tasting, Urban Winery/Wine Bar.

Varietals: Chardonnay, Merlot, Montepulciano, Napa Cab, Pinot Gris, Pinot Noir, Rose, Sangria, Tempranillo, White Blend.

Off the Rails Winery is an urban-style, pop-up winery in Temecula. It's a winery in an urban setting, but on wheels. Our historic San Francisco cable car was repurposed to be a mobile wine bar that serves our very own wine on tap.

Palumbo Family Vineyards & Winery

40150 Barksdale Circle Temecula CA 92592 951-676-7900 wineclub@palumbowines.com https://palumbowines.com

Open: Fri. thru Sun. 11 am–5 pm.

Amenities: Tasting, Tours, Wine Club.

Varietals: Cabernet Franc, Cabernet Sauvignon, Grenache, Merlot, Sangiovese, Syrah, Tannat, Viognier.

Palumbo Family Vineyards and Winery is committed to small lot, handcrafted wines from varieties that are grown on small block, sustainably farmed wine vineyards.

Parow Estate Winery

35010 Santa Rita Rd. Temecula CA 92592 951-466-8520
parowestatewinery@gmail.com https://www.parowestatewinery.com/our-vineyard-and-winery.html#/

Open: Reservations only.

Amenities: Tasting, Wine Club.

Varietals: Cabernet Franc, Cabernet Sauvignon, Merlot.

We at Parow Estate Vineyard & Winery are dedicated to developing handcrafted premium wine through sustainable agriculture without the use of artificial fertilizers or pesticides in the traditional techniques and in small batches.

Peltzer Family Cellars

40275 Calle Contento Temecula CA 92591 951-888-2008 tasting@peltzers.com
https://www.peltzerwinery.com

Open: Mon., Tue. & Thu. 12–7 pm, Wed. 12–8 pm, Fri. 12–9 pm, Sat. 11 am–10 pm, Sun. 11 am–7 pm.

Amenities: Events, Tasting, Weddings, Wine Club.

Varietals: Barbera, Cabernet Franc, Cabernet Sauvignon, Chardonnay, Malbec, Muscat Canelli, Petite Sirah, Pinot Grigio, Rose, Roussanne, Sangiovese, Sauvignon Blan, Syrah, Viognier, Zinfandel.

Our Crush House is a tasting room like no other! The building embodies owners Charlie's farming roots and Carrie's passion for design. In the Crush House, enjoy Peltzer wine tastings, bottles, and glasses.

Plateau Vineyards

20170 Sierra Soto Rd. Murrieta CA 92562 951-304-0205
https://plateauvineyards.com

Open: Reservations only.

Amenities: Events, Tasting, Wine Club.

Varietals: Albarino, Cabernet Franc, Cabernet Sauvignon, Merlot, Pinot Gris, Sauvignon Blanc, Zinfandel.

Plateau Vineyards planted its first grapevines in 1993 on a beautiful property high above the local valleys on the Santa Rosa Plateau. Our vineyard is blessed with warm sunny days, afternoon sea breezes, and cool nights, all of which allows us to grow some of the finest wine grapes in California.

Poggio Leano Winery

41309 Avenida Biona Temecula CA 92591 951-506-4617
poggioleano@gmail.com https://www.poggioleano.com/

Open: Sun. thru Tue. 11 am–6 pm, Fri. & Sat. & Sun. 11 am–8 pm.

Amenities: Tasting, Wine Club.

Varietals: Cabernet Sauvignon, Chardonnay, Malbec, Montepulciano, Moscato, Pinot Grigio, Pinot Noir, Rose, Sangiovese, Syrah.

Step onto our Sicilian-inspired estate where our family-owned and operated gem invites you to experience the essence of passion and hospitality. Every bottle of wine and every drop of extra virgin olive oil reflects our unwavering dedication to authenticity.

Poggio Leano Winery

27497 Ynez Road Temecula CA 92591 951-446-9908 poggioleano@gmail.com
https://www.visittemeculavalley.com/listing/poggio-leano-winery/1312/

Open: Tue. thru Sun. 11 am–6 pm.

Amenities: Food, Music, Lodging, Picnic, Urban Winery/Wine Bar, Tasting.

Varietals: Cabernet Sauvignon, Chardonnay, Malbec, Montepulciano, Moscato, Pinot Grigio, Pinot Noir, Rose, Sangiovese, Syrah.

Our European-style wine tasting room is located in town in the city of Temecula. Open daily with wine tasting Tuesday through Sunday 11am until 6pm, we become an upscale lounge with wine, hand-crafted spirits from 6 pm-midnight and have live entertainment Thursday-Sunday evenings.

Ponte Winery

35053 Rancho California Road Temecula CA 92591 951-694-8855
marketing@pontewinery.com https://www.pontewinery.com

Open: Mon. thru Sun. 11 am–5 pm.

Amenities: Events, Food, Lodging, Tasting, Tours, Weddings, Wine Club.

Varietals: Cabernet Sauvignon, Chardonnay, Montepulciano, Moscato, Pinot, Sangiovese, Tempranillo.

We are a boutique producer, making wines in very small batches; typically 1,500 cases per year for each variety. Compared to the California winery giants we are tiny, which allows us to concentrate on superior quality over quantity.

Raul Ramírez Bodegas Y Viñdeos

32950 Marius Way Winchester CA 92596 951-325-7728
info@raulramirezwinery.com https://raulramirezwinery.com

Open: Wed. thru Sun. 11 am–6 pm.

Amenities: Tasting, Wine Club.

Varietals: Albarino, Port, Rose, Sherry, Tempranillo, and Spanish blends.

From the heart of Temecula Valley, Raul Ramirez Bodegas Y Viñedos offers a unique selection of wines inspired by the best and most honest Spanish traditions. Growing our grape in the beautiful southern California weather is perfect for hand care of the grape we do.

Robert Renzoni Vineyards

37350 De Portola Road Temecula CA 92592 951-302-8466
wineclub@robertrenzonivineyards.com https://robertrenzonivineyards.com

Open: Mon. thru Sun. 11 am–6 pm.

Amenities: Events, Food, Tasting, Tours, Wine Club.

Varietals: Barbera, Cabernet Franc, Chardonnay, Montepulciano, Moscato, Petite Sirah, Rose, Sangiovese, Syrah, Tempranillo, Zinfandel.

Robert Renzoni Vineyards is comprised of 12 acres in the Temecula Valley that is naturally suited to grape growing. Ten of the vineyard's acres are planted to the classic Bordeaux and Italian grape varieties in 6 vineyard blocks.

Somerset Vineyards & Winery

37338 De Portola Rd. Temecula CA 92592 951-365-5522
info@somersetvineyard.com https://www.somersetvineyard.com

Open: Mon. thru Wed. 11 am–6 pm, Thu. 11 am–8:30 pm, Fri. & Sat. 11 am–9 pm, Sun. 11 am–7 pm.

Amenities: Events, Picnic, Tasting, Tours, Wine Club.

Varietals: Cabernet Franc, Cabernet Sauvignon, Muscat, Pinot Grigio, Rose, Roussanne, Sparkling Wine, Zinfandel.

Formerly Keyways Winery, the vineyard is rooted on 13 acres that bear fruit from the Rhône varietals such as Viognier, Roussanne, Grenache and Syrah as well as the Spanish Macabeo, Monastrell and Tempranillo.

South Coast Winery Resort & Spa

34843 Rancho California Road Temecula CA 92591 855-821-9431
ntuttlemondo@WineResort.com https://www.southcoastwinery.com

Open: Sun. thru Thu. 11 am–6 pm, Fri. & Sun. 11 am–8 pm.

Amenities: Events, Food, Lodging, Pool/Spa, Tasting, Weddings, Wine Club.

Varietals: Cabernet Franc, Cabernet Sauvignon, Chardonnay, Gewürztraminer, Grenache, Malbec, Merlot, Muscat Canelli, Pinot Blanc, Pinot Grigio, Pinot Noir, Port, Riesling, Rose, Sangiovese, Sauvignon Blanc, Sparkling Wine, Syrah, Tempranillo, Viognier, Zinfandel.

Surrounded by 63 acres of carefully tended vines, South Coast Winery in Temecula elevates the Southern California winery experience to Napa levels and beyond. What makes our grapes so special is the combination of the rich Southern California soil and generous Temecula Valley sunshine.

Thornton Winery

32575 Rancho California Rd. Temecula CA 92591 951-699-0099
ntuttlemondo@WineResort.com https://www.thorntonwine.com

Open: Sun. thru Thu. 11 am–7 pm, Sat. & Sun. 11 am–9 pm.

Amenities: Events, Food, Music, Tasting, Tours, Weddings, Wine Club.

Varietals: Albarino, Barbera, Chardonnay, Gewürztraminer, Malbec, Merlot, Muscat Canelli, Petite Sirah, Pinot Grigio, Rose, Sangiovese, Sauvignon Blanc, Sparkling Wine, Syrah.

Thornton Winery, the gateway to Southern California's Temecula Valley Wine Country, understands the formula for creating a premier winery that satisfies wine enthusiasts who are looking for award-winning wine, gourmet cuisine, live music, and beautiful grounds for wedding and banquet facilities.

Truffle Pig Winery

34567 Rancho California Rd. Temecula CA 92591 951-584-0000
tastingroom@trufflepigwinery.com https://trufflepigwinery.com/contact/

Open: Mon. thru Sun. 11 am–5 pm.

Amenities: Food, Music, Tasting, Tours, Weddings, Wine Club.

Varietals: Cabernet Sauvignon, Chardonnay, Chenin Blanc, Gewürztraminer, GSM, Nebbiolo, Rose, Viognier.

At Truffle Pig, we strive to uncover the finest grapes through patience, intuition, and a deep respect for the land. By carefully cultivating our vineyards and embracing the nuances of terroir, we craft wines that reflect our region's unique character.

Ultimate Vineyards

34225 Rancho California Rd. Temecula CA 92591 951-676-1711
info@mauricecarriewinery.com https://www.ultimatevineyards.com

Open: Sun. thru Thu. 11 am–5 pm, Fri. 11 am–6 pm, Sat. 11 am–6:30 pm.

Amenities: Events, Food, Picnic, Tasting, Wine Club.

Varietals: Barbera, Chardonnay, Chenin Blanc, Gewürztraminer, Malbec, Merlot, Muscat Canelli, Nebbiolo, Petite Sirah, Pinot Noir, Riesling, Rose, Sauvignon Blanc, Sparkling Wine, Syrah, Tempranillo, Zinfandel plus Maurice Car'rie and Van Roekel wines.

Ultimate Vineyards is located in the heart of Temecula Valley wine country produces wines almost exclusively from its 75-Acre estate vineyard, where a unique combination of geological and topographical features deliver fruit with extraordinary intensity, weight and voluptuousness.

Vindemia Winery

33133 Vista Del Monte Rd. Temecula CA 92591 951-760-9334
wineclub@vindemia.com https://vindemia.com

Open: Mon. thru Sun. 11 am–5 pm.

Amenities: Food, Tasting, Wine Club.

Varietals: Barbera, Cabernet Franc, Merlot, Petit Verdot, Petite Sirah, Pinot Noir, Syrah, Viognier, Zinfandel.

We are a small lot, limited production boutique winery in Temecula with a focus on sustainability. Sustainably grown. Patiently crafted.

Vitagliano Vineyards & Winery

36101 Glenoaks Rd. Bldg. D Temecula CA 92592 951-694-8466
info@vitaglianowines.com https://vitaglianowines.com

Open: Mon, Tue. Thu. & Fri. 2–7pm, Sat. 11 am–8:30 pm. Tue.

Amenities: Food, Music, Tasting, Weddings, Wine Club.

Varietals: Chardonnay, Merlot, Muscat Canelli, Pinot Grigio, Rose, Syrah, Tempranillo.

Our Estate Vineyards consists of the finest Super Tuscan varietals in Southern California. Totaling just over 10 acres of rolling hills and panoramic views we grow such varietals as Dolcetto, Cabernet Sauvignon, Pinot Grigio and Muscat Canelli.

Wiens Cellars

35055 Via Del Ponte Temecula CA 92592 951-694-9892 x 104
rosa@wienscellars.com https://www.wienscellars.com

Open: Mon. thru Sun. 10:30 am–6 pm.

Amenities: Events, Food, Music, Picnic, Tasting, Tours, Wine Club.

Varietals: Barbera, Cabernet Sauvignon, Chardonnay, Malbec, Pinot Grigio, Pinot Noir, Port, Rose, Sangiovese, Sangria, Syrah, Tempranillo.

We are Temecula's Premier Winery and Tasting Room. We produce the highest quality wines coupled with an inviting and intimate tasting experience.

Wilson Creek Winery

35960 Rancho California Road Temecula CA 92591 951-699-9463
marketing@wilsoncreekwinery.com https://www.wilsoncreekwinery.com/

Open: Sat. thru Thu. 10 am–6 pm, Fri. 10 am–8 pm.

Amenities: Events, Food, Lodging, Music, Tasting, Wine Club.

Varietals: Barbera, Cabernet Franc, Cabernet Sauvignon, Chardonnay, Grenache, , Malbec, Mourvèdre, Muscat Canelli, Petite Sirah, Pinot Noir, Roussanne, Sparkling Wine, Syrah, Viognier, Zinfandel.

Our winery seal contains the words Quality, Family and Integrity. We stand firmly by those three words as our guiding principles as we passionately create our award-winning wines.

Wine Ranch Grill & Cellars

24683 Washington Ave. Murrieta CA 92562 951-600-2800
https://thewineranch.com/

Open: Mon. thru Thu. 11:30 am–8 pm, Fri. & Sat. 11:30 am–9 pm, Sun. 10 am–8 pm.

Amenities: Restaurant, Tasting, Urban Winery/Wine Bar.

Varietals: Albarino, Cabernet Franc, Chardonnay, Chianti, GSM, Malbec, Merlot, Pinot Grigio, Riesling, Rose, Sauvignon Blanc, Sparkling, Syrah, Zinfandel.

Full service restaurant and winery offers wine tasting, American food, and craft beer by the Wiens family that begins and ends at the heart of winemaking, delicious food, in a fun inspiring full-service setting sure to make you return time and again.

Ventura County Wine Region

Ventura County on the west coast of California, separates Santa Barbara and Los Angeles. Viticulture here is usually on a relatively small scale, with most wineries making wine with grapes sourced outside of the county and serving them in a wide assortment of local Ventura county tasting rooms.

Located entirely within the western half **Malibu Coast AVA**, wines that are made from Ventura County grapes are usually full-bodied reds from Cabernet Sauvignon and Syrah. However, there are many more wineries located outside this AVA, and total for both, comes to over 20 wineries.

The terroir in Ventura County is classically mountainous. Vineyards are grown on steeper slopes surrounding the towns of Ojai and Oxnard, sometimes reaching altitudes of around 1,400 feet (420m). The rocky shale soils on these slopes have rapid drainage and cause the vines to struggle for water, resulting in lower yields of more-concentrated grapes.

Evening breezes from the nearby Pacific Ocean provide cooling relief to vineyards after warm days, and the diurnal temperature variation allows the grapes to develop rich flavors without sacrificing acidity. The cooling influence of ocean fog helps to extend the growing season.

While there are few vineyards in Ventura County, many wine-production facilities and tasting rooms can be found here, making wine with grapes from other parts of California such as Paso Robles and Monterey. Cult winery Sine Qua Non is amongst these, and makes wines from vineyards in both Santa Barbara and Ventura County.

The position of the county could have a lot to do with this: wineries here benefit from the steady stream of wine tourists travelling between the city of Los Angeles and the famed Santa Barbara wine region.

The region is also popular with, and served by conveniently located urban tasting locations, with wine varietals procured from remote vineyards or other California wine regions, that are then produced locally on site.

Ventura County Wineries A to Z

Alma Sol Winery

1321 E. Thousand Oaks Blvd. Thousand Oaks CA 91362 818-231-2749
info@almasolwinery.com https://www.almasolwinery.com/info

Open: Reservations only.

Amenities: Tasting.

Varietals: Cabernet Sauvignon, Meritage, Sauvignon Blanc.

Alma Sol is a family-owned and operated, micro-boutique winery, sourcing premium fruit from unique, quality vineyard sites in California, with a special interest and focus on the beautiful Paso Robles appellation.

Back Patio Cellars

930 Flynn Rd. Unit F Camarillo CA 93012 805-388-3457
info@backpatiocellars.com https://www.backpatiocellars.com/home.html

Open: Fri. 4–7 pm, Sat. & Sun. 1–5 pm.

Amenities: Events, Tasting, Wine Club.

Varietals: Cabernet Sauvignon, Chardonnay, Chenin Blanc, Syrah, Viognier, Zinfandel.

We make wine for ourselves, our friends, and our family. Our goal has always been simple, Quality First, if we don't love it then how could we expect you too.

Baron Herzog Wine Cellars

3201 Camino Del Sol Oxnard CA 93030 805-983-1560
https://herzogwine.com/wines

Open: Mon. thru Thu. 12–7:30 pm, Sun. 12–7:30 pm.

Amenities: Events, Food, Picnic, Tasting, Wine Club.

Varietals: Cabernet Sauvignon, Chardonnay, Chenin Blanc, Gewürztraminer, Malbec, Merlot, Pinot Grigio, Pinot Noir, Rose, Sauvignon Blanc, Zinfandel.

We are continuously expanding the boundaries and creating new and exciting wines. From globally distributed brands to boutique programs of under 100 cases, every bottle that wears the Herzog name is produced in the family's California winery.

Boccali Vineyards & Winery

3277 E. Ojai Avenue Ojai CA 93023 805-669-8688 info@boccalivineyards.com https://www.boccalivineyards.com/

Open: Sat. & Sun. 12–5 pm.

Amenities: Food, Tasting, Wine Club.

Varietals: Cabernet Sauvignon, Syrah, Viognier, Zinfandel.

Our wines are made from 100% Boccali Vineyards grapes, hand-harvested, produced onsite, and presented as nature created them, with minimal human intervention.

Camarillo Custom Crush Winery

300 S. Lewis Rd. Ste. C Camarillo CA 93012 805-484-0597 info@camarillocustomcrush.com https://www.camarillocustomcrush.com

Open: Sat. 12–5 pm, Sun. 1–5 pm.

Amenities: Events, Tasting.

Varietals: Cabernet Sauvignon, Chardonnay, Rose, Sauvignon Blanc, Syrah, Tempranillo.

Come on out to Camarillo Custom Crush on any Friday, Saturday or Sunday, to taste and purchase the best of what local has to offer. All wines are made here, for our very special custom crush clients.

Cantara Cellars

126 N. Wood Rd. #104 Camarillo CA 93010 805-484-9600 events@camarillobarrelworks.com https://camarillobarrelworks.com/about

Open: Wed. & Thu. 3–10 pm, Fri. 3–10 pm, Sat. 2–10 pm, Sun. 1–6 pm.

Amenities: Food, Private Events, Tasting, Weddings.

Varietals: Malbec, Petite Sirah, Zinfandel.

Cantara Cellars began in 2002 as a private winery at Mike and Chris Brown's Moorpark home. This culminated with the opening of a wine production facility and public tasting room in October 2007.

Casa Barranca Winery

208 E. Ojai Ave. Ojai CA 93023 805-640-1255 https://www.yelp.com/biz/casa-barranca-organic-winery-tasting-room-ojai

Open: Sun. thru Thu. 12–6 pm, Fri. & Sat. 12–7 pm.

Amenities: Tasting.

Varietals: Cabernet Franc, Chardonnay, Merlot, Pinot Noir, Sangiovese, Syrah.

We are dedicated to making only the finest natural, pure, organic wines. All the grapes used in wine making are farmed without the use of pesticides or herbicides.

Cavaletti Vineyards

165 Poindexter Ave. Suite D Moorpark CA 93021
patrick.kelley@cavalettivineyards.com https://www.cavalettivineyards.com

Open: Fri. 4–8 pm, Sat. & Sun. 12–6 pm, Mon. thru Thu. upon request.

Amenities: Tasting, Wine Club.

Varietals: Chardonnay, Grenache, Nebbiolo, Rose, Syrah, Tempranillo.

Cavaletti Vineyards is proud to be part of the small and passionate group of wineries leading a winemaking renaissance in the sunshine of Southern California. Our wines have been gaining attention since our first harvest in 2016.

Deep Sea Wine Tasting Room – Ventura

1591 Spinnaker Drive Ventura CA 93001 805-321-9463
https://www.conwayfamilywines.com/Santa-Barbara-Tasting-Room/Ventura-Tasting-Room

Open: Fri. & Sat. 11 am–9 pm, Sun. thru Thu. 11 am–8 pm.

Amenities: Events, Food, Music, Lodging, Picnic, Restaurant, Tasting, Tours, Urban Winery/Wine Bar, Weddings, Wine Club.

Varietals: Barbera, Chardonnay, Malbec, Pinot Noir, Sauvignon Blanc.

Our grapes are hand-harvested, pressed in small batches, and thoughtfully crafted by our talented winemaking team. Our labels are designed by John Conway, to celebrate our admiration for the ocean, nature, and the California coast.

End of the Road Winery

300 Fairview Road Ojai CA 9302 805-794-1565 RobertMLevin@sbcglobal.net
https://www.endoftheroadwinery.com/

Open: Reservations only.

Amenities: Tasting, Wine Club.

Varietals: Grenache, Syrah, Viognier.

While there are dozens of wineries in Ventura County now, most all of them buy their grapes from outside Ventura County and often hundreds of miles away. End of the Road Winery grows all of its own grapes and bottles its wine on the premises by hand.

Four Brix Winery & Tasting Room

2290 Eastman Avenue Suite 109 Ventura CA 93003 805-256-6006
info@fourbrixwine.com https://fourbrixwine.com/

Open: Fri. thru Sun. 12–4 pm.

Amenities: Events, Food, Music, Tasting, Tours, Urban Winery/Wine Bar.

Varietals: Barbera, Chardonnay, Grenache, Montepulciano, Nebbiolo, Pinot Noir, Sangiovese, Viognier, Zinfandel.

A craft winery located in the heart of Ventura specializing in internationally-inspired wine blends. Located at the southern end of the Central Coast, we source our grapes from Paso Robles to Santa Ynez to Ojai. Our wines are made at our Ventura winery with grapes sourced from Central Coast vineyards.

Giessinger Winery

365 Santa Clara Street Fillmore CA 93015 805-405-5557
info@giessingerwinery.com https://giessingerwinery.com

Open: Mon. & Wed. 1:30–4:30 pm, Thu. 1:30–5 pm, Fri. 1–5:30 pm, Sat. 12–6 pm, Sun. 1–5:30 pm.

Amenities: Events, Overnight RV Parking, Tasting, Wine Club.

Varietals: Cabernet Franc, Cabernet Sauvignon, Chardonnay, Petite Sirah, Pinot Gris, Sauvignon Blanc, Sparkling Wine, Zinfandel.

Our high quality, moderately priced wines bring the art of ranch Algerian beautiful California countryside in Ventura County.

Herzog Wine Cellars

3201 Camino Del Sol Oxnard CA 93030 805-983-1560
https://herzogwine.com/visit/

Open: Sun. thru Thu. 12–8 pm.

Amenities: Events, Restaurant, Tasting, Urban Winery/Wine Bar, Wine Club.

Varietals: Cabernet Sauvignon, Chardonnay, Chenin Blanc, Malbec, Merlot, Moscato, Muscat, Pinot Grigio, Pinot Noir, Rose, Sauvignon Blanc, Sparkling, Zinfandel.

Guests of Herzog Wine Cellars experience a wine making legacy spanning nine generations, in a stylish and modern winery that is nothing less than au courant. The grounds feature a lavish granite tasting bar, private tasting rooms, boutique and outdoor terrace.

Lester Family Cellars

4522 Market Street Ste. C Ventura CA 93003 562-714-9465
https://lesterfc.com

Open: Sat. & Sun. 1–6 pm and every other Friday for happy hour.

Amenities: Events, Tasting.

Varietals: Cabernet Sauvignon, Malbec, Petite Sirah, Sauvignon Blanc, Syrah, Zinfandel.

LFC is dedicated to producing small lot, handcrafted bottlings of exceptional quality varietal wines from the most premium vineyards in the Santa Barbara County. We search for vineyards which produce grapes with beautiful concentration and intense varietal character.

Magnavino Cellars

961 N. Rice Avenue Suite 5 Oxnard CA 93030 805-276-1353
https://magnavinocellars.com/

Open: Fri. 5–8 pm, Sat. & Sun. 12–6 pm.

Amenities: Events, Tasting, Wine Club.

Varietals: Cabernet Sauvignon, Chardonnay, Malbec, Petite Sirah, Pinot Noir, Sangiovese, Sparkling Wine, Syrah, Tempranillo, Zinfandel.

For many years, Robert & Barbara Wagner dreamed of opening a winery. A place that would bring friends and family together. With love, passion and hard labor, their dream became a reality in 2008, producing their first commercial vintage of wines.

Majestic Oak Vineyard

321 E. Ojai Ave. Ojai CA 93023 805-794-0272
https://www.majesticoakvineyard.com

Open: Sun. thru Thu. 12–6 pm, Fri. & Sat. 12–7 pm.

Amenities: Events, Tasting, Wine Club.

Varietals: Barbera, Cabernet Sauvignon, Grenache, Merlot, Petit Verdot, Rose, Viognier.

At Majestic Oak Vineyard, we believe that wine is for sharing with loved ones, and we treat our customers like family. We believe that wine should be enjoyed without pretension or snobbery, and we invite you to join our little family and savor our wines with delight.

Municipal Winemakers

339 N. Ventura Avenue Ventura CA 93001 805-319-6859
https://municipalwinemakers.com/pages/visit-1

Open: Sun. thru Wed. 12–8 pm, Thu. thru Sat. 12–10 pm.

Amenities: Tasting, Urban Winery/Wine Bar.

Varietals: Chardonnay, Gamay, Grenache, Petite Sirah, Pinot Noir, Riesling, Rose, Syrah.

Known for its vibrant wines, approachable ethos, and creative spirit, Muni Wine is excited to bring its signature blend of quality and community to Ventura's creative-forward neighborhood.

Nabu Wines

2649 Townsgate Road Westlake Village CA 91361 805-778-1100
events@nabuwines.com https://nabuwines.com

Open: Sun. thru Thu. 12–6 pm, Fri. & Sat. 12–11 pm.

Amenities: Events, Food, Lodging, Music, Picnic, Tasting, Tours, Weddings, Wine Club.

Varietals: Chardonnay, Chenin Blanc, Port, Sparkling Wine, Viognier.

NABU wines are crafted from amazing fruit, sustainably grown to produce both single varietal and special blend wines from Napa Valley and the Malibu Coast appellations.

Native Bloom Winery

4517 Market Street Unit 7 Ventura CA 93003 805-613-7036
natalie@nativebloomwinery.com https://www.nativebloomwinery.com/

Open: Fri. 3–8 pm, Sat. & Sun. 12–6 pm. Mon. thru Thu. reservations only.

Amenities: Tasting, Wine Club.

Varietals: Albarino, Grenache, Rose, Syrah, Viognier.

Small batch low intervention wines made in Ventura County from California Central Coast grapes. Formerly Wildflower Winery, now Native Bloom Winery! Visit our Ventura tasting room!

Ojai Vineyard, The

109 S. Montgomery St. Ojai CA 93023 805-649-1674 Help@ojaivineyard.com
https://ojaivineyard.com/tasting-room

Open: Mon. thru Sun. 12–5 pm.

Amenities: Events, Tasting.

Varietals: Barbera, Chardonnay, Grenache, Pinot Noir, Riesling, Rose, Sangiovese, Sauvignon Blanc, Syrah, Viognier.

With over 300 wines to enjoy, we welcome you to experience our tasting room in Ojai. Our highly qualified and knowledgeable staff is happy to share stories about our craft from the simplest to the most arcane.

Old Creek Ranch Winery

10024 Old Creek Road Ventura CA 93001 805-649-4132
customerservice@oldcreekranch.com https://www.oldcreekranch.com

Open: Thu. thru Mon. 11 am–5 pm.

Amenities: Food, Tasting.

Varietals: Albarino, Cabernet Franc, Cabernet Sauvignon, Chardonnay, Malbec, Pinot Gris, Pinot Noir, Rose, Sangiovese, Sauvignon Blanc, Sparkling Wine, Syrah, Tannat.

In 1981, The Whitman Family brought life to the property by starting Old Creek Ranch Winery and in 2015, the current owners, The Holguin Family, have reinvigorated the property's vineyard, orchards, and overall aesthetics of the Ranch.

Panaro Brothers Winery

4517 Market St. Suite 7 Ventura CA 93003 805-654-1577 info@panarobros.com
https://californiawineryadvisor.com/winery/Panaro-Brothers-Winery/

Open: Fri. 3–7 pm, Sat. & Sun. 11 am–7 pm.

Amenities: Tasting.

Varietals: Barbera, Cabernet Sauvignon, Chardonnay, Chenin Blanc, Gewürztraminer, Merlot, Pinot Grigio, Pinot Noir, Port, Riesling, Rose, Sangiovese, Sauvignon Blanc, Syrah, Zinfandel.

Our winemaker hand-selects the finest grapes from vineyards located in Paso Robles, Templeton, Los Alamos, Creston, Santa Ynez, San Miguel, and southern Monterey County.

Plan B Wine Cellars

3520 Arundell Circle #107 Ventura CA 93003 805-233-1453
https://planbwinecellars.com/

Open: Sat. & Sun. 1–5 pm.

Amenities: Music, Tasting, Urban Winery/Wine Bar.

Varietals: Cabernet Sauvignon, Grenache, Mourvèdre, Petite Sirah, Pinot Noir, Port, Sangiovese, Syrah.

It doesn't matter if you're a "hardcore" wine aficionado or coming for your first tasting, there's something for everyone at Plan B Wine Cellars.

Public Domain Wines

1012 West Ventura Boulevard Camarillo CA 93010 800-689-0193
info@publicdomainwines.com https://www.publicdomainwines.com/

Open: Reservations only.

Amenities: Events, Food, Tasting, Urban Winery/Wine Bar, Weddings, Wine Club.

Varietals: Cabernet Sauvignon, Chenin Blanc, Rose, Zinfandel.

Public Domain Wines consistently produces crisp, balanced and approachable wines that pair elegantly with food and are best shared with friends and family. Visit the farm to indulge in our excellent wines and the picturesque countryside that Public Domain is proud to help cultivate.

Rancho Ventavo Cellars

741 South A Street Oxnard CA 93030 805-483-8084
https://cacorks.com/winery/rancho-ventavo-cellars

Open: Fri. thru Sun. 12–5 pm.

Amenities: Tasting.

Varietals: Cabernet Franc, Cabernet Sauvignon, Mourvèdre, Petite Sirah, Syrah, Tempranillo, Zinfandel.

As a "red wine" only winery, the wines feature forward fruit qualities that offer intense, ripe fruit characteristics balanced with good acid structure, full-bodied mouth feel, and silky tannins.

Rincon Mountain Winery

4187 Carpinteria Avenue Suites #1-2 Carpinteria CA 93001 805-318-9264
hello@rinconmtn.com
https://rinconmtn.com/?fbclid=IwAR39RJJloac2o7jv0wEMpBG_6iSYasviBy0I9L
UJVoCRTf1okTw6jxHurOc

Open: Thu. thru Sun. 12–7 pm.

Amenities: Food, Tasting, Wine Club.

Varietals: Barbera, Rose, Tempranillo.

From the elegant oak profile and deep dark fruit of our Cabernet Sauvignon to the bright, clean orange blossom and honey notes of our Porch Sipper Rose, we're here to make the most flavorful wines possible.

Santa Paula Cellars

926 E. Main St. Santa Paula CA 93060 805-625-4517
https://www.yelp.com/biz/santa-paula-cellars-santa-paula?osq=Wineries

Open: Fri. 2–9 pm, Sat. 12–9 pm, Sun. 12–5 pm.

Amenities: Food, Tasting, Urban Winery/Wine Bar.

Varietals: Cabernet Sauvignon, Merlot.

We are a family-owned, small batch winery tasting room located in beautiful downtown Santa Paula.

Strey Cellars

951 N. Rice Ave. Oxnard CA 93030 805-988-1087 katie@streycellars.com
https://www.streycellars.com/

Open: Mon. Tue. Wed. Thu. thru Fri. 12–5 pm, Sat. & Sun. 12–5 pm. Reservations only.

Amenities: Events, Food, Music, Tasting, Urban Winery/Wine Bar.

Varietals: Albarino, Chardonnay, Pinot Noir, Port, Sauvignon Blanc, Viognier.

Strey wine is unequivocally a labor of love from the inside to the outside of the bottle! With meticulous attention to detail and their small case production of distinctive sparkling whites, roses, reds, and dessert wines, you will be drinking something extraordinary no matter your choice.

Sunland Vintage Winery

1321 E. Thousand Oaks Blvd. #108 Thousand Oaks CA 91362 805-379-2250
Sales@SunlandVintageWinery.com https://www.sunlandvintagewinery.com/

Open: Thu. & Fri. 6–9 pm, Sat. 1–6 pm, Sun. 1–5 pm.

Amenities: Events, Food, Music, Tasting, Weddings, Wine Club.

Varietals: Albarino, Cabernet Sauvignon, Montepulciano, Nebbiolo, Petite Sirah, Pinot Grigio, Roussanne, Sangiovese, Sparkling Wine, Tempranillo, Zinfandel.

What sets us apart from the others in Ventura County are the unique varietals we produce such as Nebbiolo, Montepulciano and Dolcetto (among others) and our special proprietary blends, Tre Ragazzi, Delicate Princes and The Goddess.

Trois le Fou Winery & Tasting Room

4522 Market Street Ste. B Ventura CA 93003 805-701-7973
info@troislefou.com https://troislefou.com/wine-tasting/

Open: Sat. & Sun. 1–6 pm.

Amenities: Events, Tasting, Urban Winery/Wine Bar, Wine Club.

Varietals: Cabernet Sauvignon, Chardonnay, Grenache, Merlot, Moscato, Mourvèdre, Petite Sirah, Rose, Syrah.

Trois le Fou is a boutique winery with a focus on producing premium Rhone and Bordeaux style wines from Paso Robles. One or two amazing tasting experiences from Trois le Fou Winery & Lester Family Cellars both located in the same building with a shared barrel room for your enjoyment.

Vino V Wines

10024 Old Creek Road Ventura CA 93001 805-207-7426 https://www.wine-searcher.com/merchant/11601-vino-v-wines

Open: Thu. thru Sun. 11 am–5 pm.

Amenities: Tasting.

Varietals: Chardonnay, Chenin Blanc, Pinot Noir, Syrah.

After 14 years making wine at two world class wineries (Mount Eden Vineyards and The Ojai Vineyard) Michael & Anita Meagher started up Vino V Wines in 2004 focusing on the goal of making distinctive wines from grapes grown in the cooler growing regions of Santa Barbara County.

Los Angeles County Wine Region

Los Angeles County is a somewhat unexpected wine region in southern California. Encompassing six different AVAs, the county is home to a diversity of terrain that leads to a wide variety of wines being produced, albeit in small quantities.

Los Angeles is the most populous county in the United States, and is half-covered with the dense urban sprawl of the city of Los Angeles. There are areas of wilderness, with the imposing Sierra Pelona mountains separate the city from the vast, dry Mojave Desert, and the Santa Monica mountains in the west of the county are too rugged for extensive development.

It is in these areas that wine production takes place. Cabernet Sauvignon and Merlot are the primary grape varieties produced, often seen combined in a Bordeaux Blend.

The Los Angeles City area and surrounding suburbs are also popular with, and served by conveniently located urban tasting locations, with wine varietals procured from remote vineyards or other California wine regions, that are then produced locally on site.

Terroir and Sub-AVAs

With almost 20 wineries, many urban tasting rooms, to choose from, Los Angeles County is home to a handful of small sub-AVAs such as the **Saddle Rock-Malibu AVA**, the eastern half of the **Malibu Coast AVA,** the **Malibu-Newton Canyon AVA** can be found in the Santa Monica mountains on the route to Santa Barbara County in the west, and the **Palos Verdes Peninsula AVA.**

These AVAs are highly respected, if little known, their high altitude protecting them from the temperature-moderating Pacific Ocean just a few miles away. Warm days followed by cold nights in these areas lead to a long growing season, and grapes are able to develop rich fruit complexity while retaining acidity.

Three more sub-AVAs **Sierra Pelona Valley AVA**, **Leona Valley AVA** and **Antelope Valley of the California High Desert AVA** –are located in the north-eastern parts of the county, spread between the northern edges of the Sierra Pelona mountains and the southern border of the Mojave Desert. These three have far more of a continental climate than the rest of Los Angeles County and are hotter, drier and far more challenging to vignerons.

It is their altitude that makes them suitable for viticulture—at around 3,000 feet (900 meters) above sea level, the vineyards enjoy a diurnal temperature variation that lengthens the ripening period, as in the Santa Monica mountains.

Despite the city's expansion and the proliferation of freeways and high-rises, there are still a few vineyards within Los Angeles itself (particularly in the eastern suburbs, which spill over into San Bernardino and Riverside counties). These vineyards have no separate AVA, and their wine is sold under the larger Los Angeles County AVA. The most notable of these is Moraga Vineyards just nine miles (14 kilometers) from the famous Hollywood sign.

History

As in much of southern California, grapes were first planted in what is now Los Angeles County in the late 18th Century by the Spanish Catholic missionary Junipero Serra at the Mission San Gabriel Archangel at San Gabriel.

But the county holds a more important distinction in Californian wine history than this. It is where a French settler named Jean-Louis Vignes planted the state's first European vines—Cabernet Franc and Sauvignon Blanc from his homeland of Bordeaux—in 1833.

By the end of the 1800s, Los Angeles County was the biggest wine region in California, and when Prohibition began in 1920, 22,000 acres (8,900 hectares) were under vine. Urban expansion since the end of World War II has led to this vineyard land being almost completely decimated by concrete, and winemaking has moved up into the hills surrounding the city.

As recently as 1950, Los Angeles County had one of the biggest agricultural industries in the United States, and was well known for growing fruit and vegetables.

Los Angeles County Wineries A to Z

Agua Dulce Vineyards

9640 Sierra Highway Agua Dulce CA 91390 661-268-7402
https://www.aguadulcewinery.com/wp

Open: Wed. thru Sun. 11 am–5:30 pm.

Amenities: Events, Lodging, Tasting, Wine Club.

Varietals: Cabernet Sauvignon, Chardonnay, Moscato, Port, Rose, Sangiovese, Syrah, Zinfandel.

Agua Dulce Winery is a 90 acre, family owned and operated, fully operational winery and vineyard, featuring daily wine tasting and tours, a gourmet gift shop, and wine sales.

Angeleno Wine Company

1646 N. Spring St. Los Angeles CA 90012 info@angelenowine.com
https://www.angelenowine.com

Open: Sat. 12–8 pm, Sun. 12–6 pm. Reservations recommended.

Amenities: Events, Picnic, Tasting, Wine Club.

Varietals: Albarino, Rose, Syrah, Tannat, Zinfandel.

With a focus on unique varietals, Angeleno Wine Co. aims to push the boundaries of what Southern California wine growing can be. Tannat, Graciano, Godello, Loureiro, Treixadura and Alicante Bouschet are some of the unique varietals that Angeleno makes into wine every year.

Antelope Valley Winery

42041 20th St. West Lancaster CA 93534 661-722-0145
cyndeedonato@gmail.com https://www.avwinery.com/

Open: Wed. thru Sun. 12–5 pm.

Amenities: Events, Food, Tasting.

Varietals: Merlot, Petit Verdot, Sangiovese, Sparkling Wine, Syrah, Tempranillo.

Antelope Valley Winery features handcrafted California red and white wines.

Barrett Cellars

114 Newgrove St. Lancaster CA 93534 661-946-3901
barrettservicesinc@gmail.com https://www.avwinegrowers.org/barrett-cellars-profile

Open: Fri. 5–10 pm, Sat. & Sun. 2–8 pm.

Amenities: Food, Tasting.

Varietals: Cabernet Sauvignon, Chardonnay, Grenache, Merlot, Pinot Noir, Sangiovese, Sauvignon Blanc, Syrah, Zinfandel.

Barrett Cellars is a wine tasting destination in the Antelope Valley, founded by a lifelong wine enthusiast John Barrett with a passion for bringing the joy and relaxation of the wine culture to others.

Blending Lab, The

5151 W. Adams Blvd. Los Angeles CA 90016 424-235-5744
info@thewineblendinglab.com https://www.thewineblendinglab.com/

Open: Mon. thru Thu. are Private Events, Fri. 5–9 pm, Sat. 2–9 pm, Sun. 2–7 pm.

Amenities: Events, Food, Tasting, Urban Winery/Wine Bar.

Varietals: GSM, Pinot, Rose, Viognier.

We understand that wine is deeply personal. That's why we're passionate about making the experience approachable and enjoyable for all. At The Blending Lab, we go beyond the traditional tasting room. We offer you something truly special: the chance to become a winemaker for a day.

Byron Blatty Wines

5122 York Blvd. Los Angeles CA 90042 323-789-6522 jenny@byronblatty.com
https://byronblatty.com/tastings

Open: Thu. & Fri. 5–9 pm, Sat. 2–5 pm, Sun. 2–6 pm.

Amenities: Events, Tasting, Urban Winery/Wine Bar, Wine Club.

Varietals: Red blends, Cabernet Sauvignon, Sangiovese, Syrah, Tempranillo.

At Byron Blatty our focus is on limited-edition, handcrafted red wines that feature sustainably farmed, family-owned vineyards in Los Angeles County. We work with over six vineyards, selecting only the most interesting, and unique expressions of Los Angeles terroir to feature in our carefully crafted wines.

Cielo Farms

31424 Mulholland Hwy. Malibu CA 90265 info@woodstockmalibu.com https://woodstockmalibu.com/

Open: Mon., Wed. & Thu. 3–8:30 pm, Fri. thru Sun. 1–8:30 pm. Closed Tue.

Amenities: Events, Music, Picnic, Tasting, Weddings, Wine Club.

Varietals: Cabernet Sauvignon, Chardonnay, Rose, Sparkling Wine, Syrah, Viognier.

As you drive through the gates of Malibu's Cielo Farms, up the winding road that seems to never end, through vineyards laden with fruit, past groves of hundred year old Tuscan olive trees, one senses a certain magic in this pristine setting.

Cornell Wine Co.

29975 Mulholland Highway Agoura CA 91301 818-575-7010 https://cornellwineco.com/

Open: Thu. 4–7 pm, Fri. 12–7 pm, Sat. & Sun. 11 am–7 pm.

Amenities: Events, Food, Tasting, Wine Bar.

Varietals: Cabernet Franc, Chardonnay, Pinot Noir, Rose, Sauvignon Blanc, Syrah.

We're a wine bar and store, located in the beautiful Santa Monica Mountains. We focus on unique, story-driven wines. We currently offer wine tastings, wine by the bottle and by the glass. We only take reservations for our signature tasting. Everything else is first come first served.

Coruce Vineyards & Winery

1055 West Columbia Way Suite #105 (& W. Avenue M) Lancaster CA 93534 805-727-3317 info@corucevineyardsandwinery.com https://www.avwinegrowers.org/coruce-vineyard-and-winery-profile

Open: Thu. thru Sat. 1–6 pm, Sun. 1–6 pm.

Amenities: Tasting.

Varietals: Chardonnay, Merlot, Sémillon, Syrah, Viognier, Zinfandel.

Coruce family has continued to expand its varietal offerings, including Malbec, Merlot, Viognier, and Symphony, a white California hybrid. The winery opened its tasting room in Lancaster, California in 2017 and invites visitors to join them on their wine adventure.

Domäne Kreger Vineyards

42257 6th Street West Suite 302 Lancaster CA 93534 661-794-2429 info@DK-wines.com https://dk-wines.com/

Open: Thu. & Fri. 3–8 pm, Sat. 12–8 pm, Sun. 12–5 pm.

Amenities: Tasting.

Varietals: Grenache, Mourvèdre, Syrah, Tempranillo.

In 2002, Don and Jamielly Kreger bought property in Littlerock, on the north slope of the San Gabriel Mountains, at almost 3000 feet elevation similar to the Pyrenees region of Europe, they planted Rioja and Rhone varietals, including 150 vines of Tempranillo, Grenache, Syrah, and Mourvèdre.

Giessinger Winery

3059 Willow Lane Westlake Village CA 91361 805-405-5557 info@giessingerwinery.com https://giessingerwinery.com

Open: Wed. 2–5 pm, Sat. & Sun. 2–6 pm.

Amenities: Events, Overnight RV Parking, Tasting, Wine Club.

Varietals: Cabernet Franc, Cabernet Sauvignon, Chardonnay, Petite Sirah, Pinot Gris, Sauvignon Blanc, Sparkling Wine, Zinfandel.

At Giessinger Winery, you will have the opportunity to experience and enjoy wine tasting in one of the most lush regions in the world.

Golden Star Vineyards

36043 106th St. East Littlerock CA 93543 661-713-6660 Lee@goldenstarvineyards.com https://www.goldenstarvineyards.com

Open: Sat. & Sun. 12–6 pm.

Amenities: Tasting, Wine Club.

Varietals: Cabernet Sauvignon, Pinot Noir, Syrah, Viognier, Zinfandel.

We make every effort to follow sustainable farming practices and a minimalist approach to winemaking, as our focus is on small lot handcrafted premium wines. After 12-18 months, the wine is bottled and held for a minimum of 6 months before its release to our wine club and customers.

Grafted Cellars Restaurant & Winery Tasting Room

135 W. 1st St. Claremont CA 91711 909-312-7359 info@graftedcellars.com https://graftedcellarswinery.com/

Open: Tue. thru Thu. 4–10 pm, Fri. & Sat. 12–11 pm, Sun. 12–9 pm.

Amenities: Events, Restaurant, Tasting, Urban Winery/Wine Bar, Wine Club.

Varietals: Cabernet Franc, Cabernet Sauvignon, Chardonnay, Chenin Blanc, Gewürztraminer, Grenache, Pinot Grigio, Pinot Noir.

Welcome to the best restaurant in Claremont! Grafted Cellars Winery and Restaurant is an urban Winery that makes delicious craft wines sourced from sustainable and non-commercially farmed vineyards. At our restaurant you can enjoy all the benefits of a wine club with delicious foods to pair with.

Hoi Polloi Winery

621 N. Niagara St. Burbank CA 91505 818-929-3684 info@hoipolloiwinery.com https://www.hoipolloiwinery.com/contact/

Open: Thu. thru Sat. 5–10 pm, Sun. 2–6 pm.

Amenities: Tasting, Wine Club.

Varietals: Cabernet Sauvignon, Chardonnay, Grenache, Pinot Noir, Rose, Syrah.

Our micro-scale production means every barrel we produce gets our full hands-on attention, something large scale wineries simply cannot do. Our wines are more than just pressed grapes. Into our bottles, we squeeze our collective effort, sparse savings and a deep, desperate desire for profitability.

Le Vigne Winery

2325 E. 55th Street Vernon CA 90058 323-689-7005 lvla@levignewinery.com https://www.levignewinery.com/le-vigne-la

Open: Wed. & Sun. 11:30 am–5 pm, Thu. thru Sat. 11:30 am–7 pm.

Amenities: Events, Food, Tasting, Urban Winery/Wine Bar, Wine Club.

Varietals: Cabernet Franc, Cabernet Sauvignon, Chardonnay, Grenache, Malbec, Merlot, Mourvèdre, Petite Sirah, Sangiovese, Sparkling, Syrah.

Safely tucked away inside the vast industrial area of Vernon, California, you will find a hidden gem. Our authentic Tasting Room & Market reminds visitors of Old World Italy, to quickly forget the hustle and bustle outside. It's rustic, spacious, and features a large selection of artisan cheese and accoutrements.

Malibu Wines & Beer Garden

23130 Sherman Way West Hills CA 91307 818-578-4146
info@malibufamilywines.com https://www.malibufamilywines.com/about-us/

Open: Sun. thru Thu. 12–7 pm, Fri. & Sat. 12–9 pm.

Amenities: Events, Food, Tasting, Wine Club.

Varietals: Cabernet Sauvignon, Chardonnay, Grenache, Malbec, Merlot, Moscato, Petit Verdot, Port, Riesling, Rose, Sauvignon Blanc, Sparkling Wine, Syrah, Zinfandel.

Malibu Family Wines specializes in crafting unforgettable experiences around premium wines. With 70,000 vines on the 1,000 acre Semler Family ranch nestled in the hills of Malibu, Malibu Family Wines produces over 12 different varietals between the Semler and Saddlerock brands.

Moraga Bel Air

650 N. Sepulveda Blvd. Los Angeles CA 90049 831-600-6263
Philip@MoragaBelair.com https://www.moragabelair.com/pages/the-vineyard

Open: Reservations only.

Amenities: Cave, Food, Tasting, Tours.

Varietals: Cabernet Franc, Cabernet Sauvignon, Merlot, Petit Verdot, Sauvignon Blanc grapes used for Blends.

The overriding objective of grape growing practices at Moraga Vineyards is to produce the best possible fruit in a sustainable manner. Most of the vineyard is closely spaced on sloping hillsides that are inaccessible to tractors and other equipment.

Pagter Brothers Winery

24338 Main Street Santa Clarita CA 91321 661-476-5627 info@pagterbros.com
https://www.pagterbros.com/index.html

Open: Thu. & Fri. 5–10 pm, Sat. 12–10 pm, Sun. 12–6 pm.

Amenities: Events, Tasting, Wine Club.

Varietals: Cabernet, Grenache, Petite Sirah, Pinot Noir, Rose, Tempranillo,
Viognier, Zinfandel.

Pagter Brothers Winery is a small batch boutique winery located in Valencia
California. We primarily source our grapes from select vineyards in Paso Robles
and Santa Ynez, but are always on the lookout for premium fruit from coveted
vineyards from other terroirs.

Pulchella Winery

24261 Main Street Newhall CA 91321 661-799-9463
customerservice@pulchellawinery.com https://pulchellawinery.com/

Open: Thu. 4–9 pm, Fri. & Sat. 4–10 pm, Sun. 12–5 pm.

Amenities: Picnic, Tasting, Wine Club.

Varietals: Pinot Noir, Rose, Syrah, Tannat, Viognier, Zinfandel.

The atmosphere of the tasting room is very comfortable, laid back and relaxing
with ample seating. No reservations are required for groups of 8 or less. Larger
groups please call or email us for reservations.

Reyes Winery

10262 Sierra Highway Santa Clarita CA 91390 661-268-1865
info@ReyesWinery.com https://reyeswinery.com/

Open: Sat. & Sun. 11 am–5 pm.

Amenities: Events, Tasting, Wine Club.

Varietals: Cabernet Sauvignon, Merlot, Syrah.

The winery is located in Northern Los Angeles County in the small town of Agua
Dulce northeast of the Santa Clarita Valley. Reyes Winery has already won 350
medals and awards on its wines during the last nine years since the wines have
been available commercially.

Rosenthal – The Malibu Estate

18741 Pacific Coast Highway Malibu CA 90265 310-456-1392
tastingroom@rosenthalestatewines.com
https://rosenthalestatewines.com/malibu-vineyard

Open: Wed. thru Fri. 12–7 pm, Sat. 11 am–8 pm, Sun. 11 am–7 pm.

Amenities: Events, Food, Music, Picnic, Tasting, Wine Club.

Varietals: Cabernet Franc, Cabernet Sauvignon, Chardonnay, Merlot, Petit Verdot, Rose, Viognier.

Escape 1,400 feet up into the hills of Malibu, and join us at the spectacular Rosenthal–The Malibu Estate vineyard for a tour and wine tasting. Here on this sprawling 250-acre property, enjoy a premium flight of Rosenthal and Surfrider wines, while surrounded by the beautiful scenery.

San Antonio Winery

737 Lamar Street Los Angeles CA 90031 323-330-8771
support@sanantoniovineyards.com
https://sanantoniowinery.com/locations/los-angeles

Open: Reservations only at Stefano Cellar Group Wine Tasting Experience.

Amenities: Events, Food, Music, Tasting, Wine Club.

Varietals: Cabernet Franc, Cabernet Sauvignon, Chardonnay, Merlot, Moscato, Pinot Noir, Rose, Sauvignon Blanc, Viognier, Zinfandel.

San Antonio Winery remains the oldest and largest producing winery in Los Angeles with over 100 years of winemaking, making it an essential component of the city's cultural and historical landscape. The winery is the last vestige of the rich winemaking tradition of greater Los Angeles.

Stephen Hemmert Wines

44732 Yucca Ave. Lancaster CA 93534 805-727-3317
stephenhemmertwines@gmail.com https://www.avwinegrowers.org/stephen-hemmert-wines-profile

Open: Fri. 5–9 pm, Sat. & Sun. 2–6 pm.

Amenities: Events, Tasting, Wine Club.

Varietals: Chardonnay, Grenache, Merlot, Sauvignon Blanc, Syrah, Tannat, Tempranillo, Zinfandel.

Stephen Hemmert Wines was founded by Stephen Hemmert and his partner and fiancée, Nicole St. Julian, in 2014. The company is based in Lancaster, and focuses on producing small batches of unique and rare varietal wines from various sources in California.

Strange Family Vineyards

3939 Cross Creek Road Suite B100 Malibu CA 90265 213-716-0795
maria@strangefamilyvineyards.com https://www.strangefamilyvineyards.com/

Open: Mon. thru Thu. 12–5 pm, Fri. thru Sun. 12–6 pm. Reservations strongly encouraged.

Amenities: Events, Tasting, Wine Club.

Varietals: Chardonnay, Pinot Noir, Sparkling Wine, Syrah.

Strange Family Vineyards produces exceptional Pinot Noir and Chardonnay from our estate in the famed Sta Rita Hills AVA of Santa Barbara County, crafted to embrace the distinct characteristics of our vineyard and region.

Orange County Wine Region

While Orange County wineries aren't quite as famous as the beautiful beaches and prime shopping locations, the area is nevertheless home to a well-established Southern Californian wine-making tradition and culture.

With a warm and temperate climate that favors the cultivation of grapes, California currently produces around 90 percent of all American-made wine. Furthermore, it supplies around 60 percent of all wine consumed in the US, as well as steadily gaining traction in the international wine industry.

Not to be confused with Orange County in Florida, an up-and-coming US wine-making region in its own right, wineries in Orange County are well-known for their quality wines, pleasant atmosphere, and great service.

With a handful of wineries to choose from, the region is also popular with, and served by conveniently located urban tasting locations, with wine varietals procured from remote vineyards or other California wine regions, that are then produced locally on site.

Orange County has no AVAs of its own, and instead, is encompassed in the original South Coast AVA.

Orange County Wineries A to Z

A Stone's Throw Winery

29943 Camino Capistrano San Juan Capistrano CA 92675 949-364-2063
Events@giracci.com https://astonesthrowwinery.com/proprietors

Open: Mon. thru Sat. by Reservations only.

Amenities: Events, Tasting, Weddings, Wine Club.

Varietals: Cabernet Sauvignon, Chardonnay, Sangiovese, Sparkling Wine, Syrah, Zinfandel.

This historic home now serves as the tasting room for Hamilton Oaks' award-winning wines, and they planted 4 rows of Mission vines, bringing a little bit of local history to the site. Mission vines were brought to the San Juan Capistrano Mission from Spain by Father Serra, California's premier winegrower.

Bellante Family Winery

23854 Via Fabricante Unit D-2 Mission Viejo CA 92691 949-716-6677
info@bellantefamilywinery.com https://www.bellantefamilywinery.com

Open: Fri. 5–9 pm, Sat. 12–7 pm, Sun. 12–5 pm.

Amenities: Events, Food, Music, Tasting, Wine Club.

Varietals: Grenache, Mourvèdre, Pinot Noir, Syrah, Viognier.

We have been making world class, small lot, hand crafted, age worthy wines from Santa Barbara County fruit since 2000.

Bianchi Winery

496 N. Coast Highway Laguna Beach CA 92651 949-964-69100
cristina@bianchiwine.com https://www.bianchiwine.com

Open: Mon. thru Thu. 4–8 pm, Fri. 2–9 pm, Sat. 11:30 am–9 pm, Sun. 11:30 am–7 pm.

Amenities: Events, Lodging, Music, Tasting, Wine Club.

Varietals: Cabernet Sauvignon, Chardonnay, Merlot, Petite Sirah, Pinot Grigio, Pinot Noir, Port, Rose, Sangiovese, Sauvignon Blanc, Sparkling Wine.

Dedicated to producing premium quality wines using the best grapes of the Central Coast. The Bianchi Family invites you to enjoy our Chardonnay, Sauvignon Blanc, Pinot Grigio, Cabernet Sauvignon, Pinot Noir, Merlot, Petite Sirah, and many blends.

Giracci Vineyards & Farms

16162 Jackson Ranch Rd. Silverado CA 92676 714-602-1109
https://www.giracci.com

Open: Fri. thru Sun. 11 am–5 pm. Reservations only.

Amenities: Events, Food, Tasting, Weddings, Wine Club.

Varietals: Barbera, Cabernet Sauvignon, Chardonnay, Merlot, Pinot Noir, Sangiovese, Sparkling Wine, Syrah, Zinfandel.

Conveniently located in the heart of Orange County, the Silverado locale transports you to another place and time. Sprawling vineyards, whitewashed fences, vintage historic buildings and barns, riding arenas, trails and streams with magnificent, mature old oak trees paint the landscape.

Laguna Canyon Winery

2133 Laguna Canyon Rd. Laguna Beach CA 92651 949-715-9463
info@lagunacanyonwinery.com https://lagunacanyonwinery.com

Open: Wed. thru Fri. 12–5 pm, Sat. & Sun. 12–5 pm. Reservations only.

Amenities: Events, Food, Tasting, Wine Club.

Varietals: Cabernet Sauvignon, Chardonnay, Grenache, Malbec, Moscato, Petite Sirah, Pinot Grigio, Rose, Sauvignon Blanc, Sparkling Wine, Syrah.

A unique wine tasting at one of Orange County's hidden gems in Laguna Beach. Whether you book a corporate or Private Events, visit us for a daytime wine tasting or join the wine club—we hope you will savor the aroma and flavor of our expressive and carefully crafted boutique wines.

Modern Cellar, The

9969 Walker St. Cypress CA 90630 714-699-1138 hello@moderncellarwine.com
https://moderncellarwine.com/

Open: Tue. thru Thu. 8 am–6 pm, Fri. & Sat. 8 am–8 pm, Sun. 8 am–1:30 pm.

Amenities: Events, Restaurant, Tasting, Urban Winery/Wine Bar, Wine Club.

Varietals: Charcuterie Wine Tasting.

We offer a variety of experiences for both wine connoisseurs and newcomers, including tastings, wine pairings, and educational workshops. Whether you're looking for a fun night out with friends or want to learn more about wine, we have an event for you.

Newport Beach Vineyards & Winery

2128 Mesa Drive Newport Beach CA 92660 949-645-2200 Info@nbwine.com http://www.nbwine.com

Open: Reservations only.

Amenities: Events, Food, Tasting, Tours, Weddings, Wine Club.

Varietals: Chardonnay, Cuvee, Pinot Noir, Rose, Sauvignon Blanc, Zinfandel.

Since 2001 we have been growing, harvesting, and maturing our award-winning wines on property nestled in the Upper Newport Bay. We specialize in hosting special events for groups of all types, with the exception of large wedding ceremonies. Let us provide the foundation for your occasion.

Orange Coast Winery

869 W. 16th St. Newport Beach CA 92663 949-645-0400 info@orangecoastwinery.com https://www.orangecoastwinery.com

Open: Thu. 2–7 pm, Fri. & Sat. 2–8 pm, Sun. 2–7 pm.

Amenities: Events, Tasting, Wine Club.

Varietals: Cabernet Sauvignon, Malbec, Merlot, Petite Sirah, Rose, Zinfandel.

We are a local boutique winery in Newport Beach offering quality wine made with the finest grapes sourced from Temecula Valley, Paso Robles and Lodi, California.

Pali Wine Co.

500 S. Anaheim Blvd. Unit C Anaheim CA 92805 714-486-0922 packingdistrict@paliwineco.com https://paliwineco.com/pages/locations-outposts

Open: Mon. thru Thu. 4–10 pm, Fri. 2 pm–12 am, Sat. 11 am–12 am, Sun. 2 pm–9 pm.

Amenities: Tasting, Urban Winery/Wine Bar.

Varietals: Cabernet Sauvignon, Chardonnay, Cuvee, Pinot Noir.

Pali Wine Co. is about good times, an essential ingredient to health and wellness. It's impossible to imagine our favorite nights with friends and family, our most memorable meals, and our fondest memories without a glass of fine wine.

Seal Beach Winery

3387 Cerritos Avenue Los Alamitos CA 90720 562-594-5800
info@sealbeachwinery.com https://www.sealbeachwinery.com

Open: Wed. & Thu. 2–9 pm, Fri. 2–10 pm, Sat. 1–10 pm, Sun. 1–7 pm.

Amenities: Events, Tasting, Wine Club.

Varietals: Cabernet Sauvignon, Chardonnay, Malbec, Muscat, Petit Verdot, Pinot, Pinot Noir, Rose, Sangiovese, Syrah, Tempranillo.

Our winemaker Michael Dawson has a long history of enjoying and collecting some of the world's best wines. He is also an alumnus of the fabled enology and viticulture program at UC Davis, which has educated some of California's most sought after stars.

San Bernardino County Wine Region

Cucamonga Valley AVA

The Cucamonga Valley AVA is located in the San Bernardino and Riverside counties in the eastern sprawl of Los Angeles. Once home to one of the largest areas under vine in California, Cucamonga Valley is now the site of just a handful of vineyards producing old-vine Zinfandel and port-style wines in the middle of suburbia.

The AVA covers the southern foothills of the imposing San Gabriel Mountain range and extends down to the Santa Ana River, which flows through the northwest corner of Riverside County. At establishment in 1995, Cucamonga Valley covers 109,400 acres (44,272 hectares), although with the proximity to the city of Los Angeles, small vineyards are now found nestled among houses, factories and airports.

Less than 1,000 acres (405 hectares) of vineyards remain, and these are under threat from the ongoing demand for land for development. A few hardy souls remain in the area producing rich, age-worthy wines made from Zinfandel, Mourvèdre and Syrah and fortified wines made in the Sherry style.

Terroir and AVAs

Soils in the hot, desert-like valley are rocky and sandy, allowing for excellent drainage. The lack of water in the soils and the heat of the region mean that the grapes produced by the vines are smaller than normal, with thicker skins and more-concentrated flavors. This leads to a typical Cucamonga Valley wine style that is big and bold with firm, ripe tannins.

The climate here is Mediterranean with hot, dry summers and cool, wet winters. Temperatures regularly reach 104 Fahrenheit (40 Celsius) throughout the summer. The region is impacted by the Santa Anas winds, of which can reach up to 80 miles per hour (128 km/hr). This is potentially detrimental throughout flowering and fruitset in the springtime.

History

The valley was once an agricultural mecca, and at the beginning of Prohibition in 1920 had more acreage under vine than both Sonoma and Napa counties. Those days are long gone, and the regions has a handful of wineries to choose from.

Vines were first planted in Cucamonga in the 1830s, and the discovery of the region as a premium site for viticulture is largely credited to an Italian immigrant named Secondo Guasti from the wine-growing region of Piedmont. Recognizing the potential of the soils and the climate, he pioneered grape growing here with plantations of Zinfandel.

By 1917 the Cucamonga-Guasti vineyards spanned over 20,000 acres, and Secondo Guasti was advertising his vineyard as "The Largest in the World." When Prohibition began in 1920, the Cucamonga Valley produced more wine grapes than Napa County and Sonoma County combined.

Grape growing continued throughout Prohibition and Cucamonga Zinfandel grapes were shipped all across the state for home winemaking, which was permitted under national law during this time. Prohibition finally ended in 1933. Even until the 1950s, the larger Los Angeles area was one of the largest agricultural areas in the United States.

Yucaipa Valley AVA

The Yucaipa Valley AVA was approved in 2024 and is a region of rolling hills in the foothills of the San Bernardino Mountains and includes the incorporated municipalities of Yucaipa and Calimesa and the unincorporated area of Oak Glen. The climate of the AVA as a hot, dry climate suitable for growing grape varietals such as Cabernet Sauvignon, Merlot, Zinfandel, Syrah, Malbec, Nebbiolo, Barbera, and Petite Sirah.

Elevations within the Yucaipa Valley AVA range from 2,000 to 4,600 feet where sunlight becomes more concentrated at high elevations. As a result, grapes receive a "tan," which results in thicker skin than the same varietals grown at lower elevations. The thick skins contribute to the color and tannin levels of the resulting wine and protect developing grapes from the dramatic climate shifts that can occur in high altitude vineyards.

San Bernardino County Wineries A to Z

Argonza Cellars

13788 Roswell Avenue Suite 166 Chino CA 91710 909-522-0615
argonzacellars@gmail.com https://www.argonzacellars.com/about

Open: Tue. thru Sat. 5–9 pm.

Amenities: Tasting.

Varietals: Cabernet Franc, Cabernet Sauvignon, Malbec, Merlot, Pinot Noir, Zinfandel.

Argonza Cellars has worked to assemble and nurture a team that understands how to bring great wine to the table. While mostly a family owned and operated winery, many industry experts have joined Emerald Argonza and his wife Rowena.

Biane Wine

10013 8th St. Suite T Rancho Cucamonga, CA 91730 909-980-7987
info@bianewine.com https://www.bianewine.com/

Open: Thu. thru Sun. 12–6 pm. Reservations only.

Amenities: Food, Tasting, Tours, Weddings, Wine Club.

Varietals: Cabernet Sauvignon, Chardonnay, Meritage, Rose, Sangiovese, Zinfandel.

The family's home is the Biane Brothers Winery, located on the property of the former Pierre Biane Winery and California Bonded Winery #1, one of the oldest-standing California wineries and the birthplace of the California wine industry.

Galleano Winery

4231 Wineville Rd. Mira Loma CA 91752 951-685-5376
info@galleanowinery.com https://www.galleanowinery.com

Open: Tue. thru Sun. 9 am–5 pm.

Amenities: Events, Picnic, Tasting, Tours.

Varietals: Cabernet Sauvignon, Chardonnay, Chianti, Petite Sirah, Pinot Gris, Port, Riesling, Rose, Sherry, Sparkling Wine, Zinfandel.

The Historic Galleano Winery was founded in 1927 by Domenico Galleano and is open daily for wine flights, wines by the glass, and wines by the bottle. Galleano is the oldest Prohibition-era winery in the Cucamonga Valley still owned by the family and operating at its original location.

Joseph Filippi Winery

12467 Base Line Road Rancho Cucamonga CA 91739 909-899-5755
info@josephfilippiwinery.com https://cacorks.com/winery/joseph-flilppi-winery

Open: Tue. 12–8 pm, Wed. & Thu. 12–6 pm, Fri. & Sat. 12–7 pm, Sun. 12–6 pm.

Amenities: Events, Tasting.

Varietals: Cabernet Franc, Cabernet Sauvignon, Chardonnay Grenache, Merlot, Petite Sirah, Pinot Grigio, Port, Rose, Sangiovese, Sparkling Wine, Syrah, Zinfandel.

At Joseph Filippi Winery, history and tradition of the Filippi winegrowing family continues and flourishes today with each new vintage as 4th generation Joseph 'J.P.' Filippi and his son Jared build upon over 90 years in the historic Cucamonga-Guasti winegrowing area.

North Cork Vineyard & Winery

9677 Yucaipa Ridge Rd. Yucaipa CA 92399 909-838-0721
northcorkvineyard@gmail.com https://north-cork-vineyard-winery.square.site

Open: Fri. 5–10:30 pm, Sat. 4–10:30 pm, Sun. 4–9 pm.

Amenities: Food, Events, Music, Tasting, Weddings.

Varietals: Barbera, Chardonnay, Sangiovese Zinfandel.

We are a locally owned and operated boutique vineyard & winery. Situated on the picturesque North Bench of Yucaipa, we offer outdoor wine tastings with magnificent views of the valleys below.

Rancho de Philo Winery

10050 Wilson Ave. Alta Loma CA 91737 909-987-4208
info@ranchodephilo.com https://www.ranchodephilo.com

Open: For 9 days only every year from the second Saturday to the third Sunday every November. Go to their website Contact page for exact days and contact them by email for the operating hours.

Amenities: Tasting, Wine Club.

Varietals: Petite Sirah, Sherry, Viognier.

While our Triple Cream Sherry remains at the heart of Rancho de Philo, we're proud to offer a Viognier and Petite Sirah, sourced from celebrated vineyards in Lodi, California that reflect the spirit, care, and tradition of the Biane's family winemaking heritage dating back to 1832.

San Antonio Winery

2802 S. Milliken Avenue Ontario CA 91761 909-947-3995
support@sanantoniovineyards.com
https://sanantoniowinery.com/locations/los-angeles

Open: Mon., Tue. & Thu. 9 am–6 pm, Fri. thru Sun. 9 am–7 pm.

Amenities: Events, Food, Tasting, Wine Club.

Varietals: Cabernet Franc, Cabernet Sauvignon, Chardonnay, Merlot, Moscato, Pinot Noir, Rose, Sauvignon Blanc, Viognier, Zinfandel.

Named the Inland Empire's premier wine destination, the San Antonio Winery Ontario Tasting Room & Gift Shop has been faithfully serving guests for over 40 years. With a prestigious tasting room, and a casual Country Patio, the winery is Ontario's hidden gem.

Suveg Cellars

12132 California St. Yucaipa CA 92399 909-768-2220
https://www.suvegcellars.com/

Open: Mon. thru Thu. 4–8 pm, Fri. 4–8 pm, Sat. 12–10 pm, Sun. 12–8 pm.

Amenities: Events, Food, Music, Tasting, Wine Club.

Varietals: Albarino, Cabernet Sauvignon, Malbec, Mourvèdre, Nebbiolo.

Suveg Cellars wines are inspired by classic expressions of French and Italian varietals from heritage regions throughout both countries. Whether you are looking for dry, light, medium, or full bodied wines, we know you'll find a Suveg Cellars wine that matches your palate.

Sycamore Ranch Vineyard & Winery

174 N. Dart Canyon Crestline CA 92325 909-338-1725
eak@sycamoreranch.com https://www.sycamoreranch.com

Open: Reservations only on Fri. at 1 & 3 pm, Sat. & Sun. at 11 am, 1 & 3 pm.

Amenities: Events, Food, Picnic, Tasting, Wine Club.

Varietals: Cabernet Sauvignon, Grenache, Merlot, Mourvèdre, Petite Sirah, Rose, Roussanne, Syrah, Viognier.

Winemaker Richard Krumwiede and his willing collaborators, have created a unique destination winery, producing award winning Rhone and Bordeaux varietals.

California Wine Grapes & Varietals

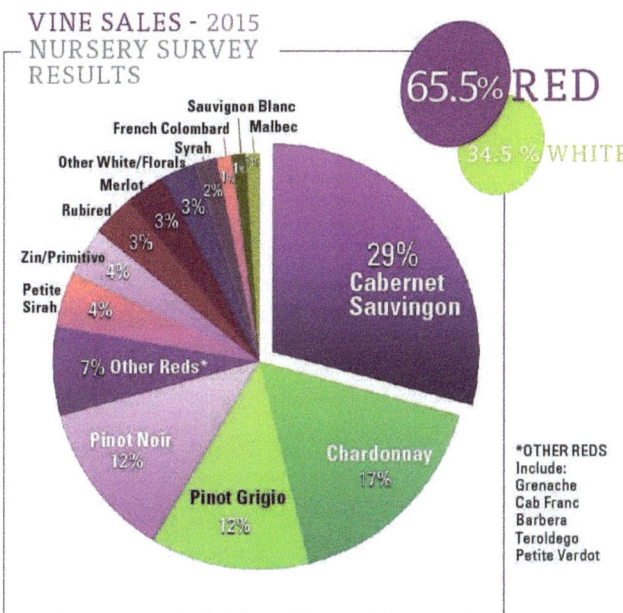

VINE SALES - 2015 NURSERY SURVEY RESULTS

65.5% RED
34.5% WHITE

Sauvignon Blanc
French Colombard | Malbec
Syrah
Other White/Florals
Merlot
Rubired
Zin/Primitivo
Petite Sirah

29% Cabernet Sauvingon

2%
3%
3%
3%
4%
4%
7% Other Reds*
Pinot Noir 12%
Pinot Grigio 12%
Chardonnay 17%

*OTHER REDS
Include:
Grenache
Cab Franc
Barbera
Teroldego
Petite Verdot

Over time, a handful of wine grape varieties have come to dominate the winemaking world. Red wine grapes and white wine grape varietals differ in their predominant aroma, sugar levels, natural acidity, and level of tannins.

Wine grape varieties are the heart and soul of every bottle, contributing distinct flavors, aromas, and characteristics unique to each varietal. Each grape's individuality is shaped not only by its inherent genetic traits, but also by the region, sub-region, and specific microclimate in which it is grown.

The concept of terroir, or the environmental factors that influence a wine's character, plays a significant role in this process. Factors such as soil composition, altitude, and climate can dramatically alter the taste and aroma of a particular grape variety, leading to a diverse range of expressions in the resulting wines.

With that noted, here are the lists of the most popular California white and red wine varietals.

8 Most Popular White Wine Grapes in California

Chardonnay
Chenin Blanc
Muscat or Moscato
Pinot Grigio
Riesling
Sauvignon Blanc
Sémillon
Viognier

10 Most Popular Red Wine Grapes in California

Cabernet Franc
Cabernet Sauvignon
Grenache
Malbec
Merlot
Petit Sirah
Pinot Noir
Sangiovese
Syrah
Zinfandel

California Wine Varietals

We chose *not* to separate this list of wines from A to Z below into white, red, or other general wine category sections because the reader may not know beforehand whether a wine is a red or a white one when searching for it. For that reason, we kept the reds and whites mixed below, and instead used the lists above for the purpose of identifying the major grape varietals used for red or white wines.

A note about wine varietal names: New World wines are generally labeled by varietal, where Old World wines are labeled by region (i.e., Bordeaux wine refers to a wine made in the Bordeaux region of France. Cabernet Sauvignon and Merlot are two varietals grown in Bordeaux). There are thousands of wine varietals in the world, but here is a short list of popular varietals.

The most popular California wine varietals listed below in alphabetical order, and the most important wine grape varietals used for making wine throughout the state are Chardonnay, Cabernet Sauvignon, Merlot, Syrah, Zinfandel, Sauvignon Blanc, and Pinot Noir.

Albariño

Alberino is an interesting grape that traces its origin to the Iberian Peninsula, and continues to flourish today in Spain. The hallmarks of this aromatic white wine are crispness and dryness with excellent balance.

Barbera

Barbera is a red wine grape found primarily in Italy's Piedmont region. It produces hearty red wines with deep ruby colors, full body and low tannin levels.

Bordeaux

Bordeaux wine is produced in the Bordeaux region of southwest France, around the city of on the Garonne River.

Cabernet Franc

Cabernet Franc is much lighter than Cabernet Sauvignon and is a vivid, fair red. It contributes a peppery scent to blends with more full-bodied grapes. Depending on the region it is grown in and the type of wine, other scents include raspberry, tobacco, and cassis—sometimes, even violets.

Cabernet Sauvignon

Cabernet Sauvignon is acknowledged as the "king" of red grapes. Cabernet Sauvignon grapes are complex. Essences of black currants, green olives, herbs, bell peppers or blends of the latter can be discerned from this grape's versatile wine.

Chardonnay

Chardonnay is among the most widely planted grape variety due to its popularity and versatility. Many vineyards make several varieties of Chardonnay wines, ranging from crisp and refreshing to complex and rich, each type as indulgent as the last.

Chenin Blanc

Chenin Blanc is a white wine with fresh, delicate floral characteristics. It grows well in warmer climates and produces light, well- balanced wines ranging from dry to off-dry (slightly sweet) styles.

Dolcetto

This red wine grape is found almost exclusively in Italy's Piedmont region. It produces light and fruity wine.

French Colombard

Colombard (also known as French Colombard in North America) is a white French wine grape variety that may be the offspring of Chenin blanc and Gouais blanc.

Gewürztraminer

Gewürztraminer is a white German wine that produced distinctive wines rich in spicy aromas and full flavors, ranging from dry to sweet.

Grenache

Grenache or Garnacha is one of the most widely planted red wine grape varieties in the world. It is generally spicy, berry-flavored and soft on the palate and produces wine with a relatively high alcohol content, but it needs careful control of yields for best results.

Malbec

The Malbec grape is thin-skinned, ripens mid-season and brings abundant tannin, a rich color, and a particular plum-like flavor that adds intricacy to claret blends of wine. These inky, dark grapes require more sun and warmth than both the Cabernet Sauvignon and Merlot to develop, producing tough tannins.

Marsanne

Marsanne is a white wine grape, most commonly found in the Northern Rhône region. It is often blended with Roussanne.

Merlot

Though customarily used as a blending wine, Merlot gained admiration for its singularity in the early seventies. Merlot wines radiate divine cherry-like aromas with hints of herbaceousness that can be compared to the Cabernet grape's greenery flavors. However, Merlot's tannins are softer than those found in Cabernet grapes therefore the wines are drinkable much earlier.

Moscato

Moscato is a fragrant sweet wine from Italy that is often characterized by bright and inviting flavors of Meyer lemon, mandarin orange, pear, orange blossom .

Mourvèdre

This warm-weather, red wine grape is common in Southern France's Rhone Valley. Rich in color with early aromas, often blended with Syrah.

Muscat Canelli

Muscat Canelli is perhaps one of the most delicious grapes to snack on in the entire Vitis Vinifera species. Muscat is a grape variety with many variants of itself as well, and in particular is a grape named after the town of Canelli (Città di Canelli) in North-East Italy in the larger winemaking region of Piedmont.

Nebbiolo

Quite perversely, Nebbiolo is one of the first varieties to bud yet the last variety to ripen, harvesting mid to late October. As they age, the wines can be characterized by a brick-orange hue at the rim of the glass. When maturing, scents and flavors can include violets, tar, wild herbs, cherries, raspberries, truffles, tobacco, and prunes. These wines often require years of aging in order to equalize the intensity of the tannins with other qualities of the wine.

Petite Sirah

"Petite" in the name of this grape refers to the size of it berries—not the vine, which is particularly robust. The grapes' tightly packed clusters can be prone to rotting in rainy environments which could make harvesting this variety difficult. The petite berries create a high skin to juice ratio; this can produce very tannic wines if the juice goes through a lengthy maceration period. In the presence of new oak barrels, the wine can develop an aroma of melted chocolate.

Petit Verdot

Petit Verdot is a variety of red wine grape. It is primarily used in classic Bordeaux and Cabernet Sauvignon blends, helping to 'stiffen' the mid palate of these mixes. This grape ripens much later than the other varieties in which eventually diminished its fancy in its home region. When it finally does ripen, it is added in slight quantities to enhance the tannin, color, and flavor of the blend.

Pinot Blanc

Pinot Blanc is a white wine grape. It is a point genetic mutation of Pinot noir. Pinot noir is genetically unstable and will occasionally experience a point mutation in which a vine bears all black fruit except for one cane which produces white fruit.

Pinot Grigio (Pinot Gris)

Pinot Grigio (or Pinot Gris) is a white wine grape variety with fruit that normally has a grayish-blue hue, as its name explains ("gris" meaning "grey" in French); however, the grape can have a brownish pink to black, and even white, color. Pinot Gris wines are typically light to medium bodied with a yellow to copper-pink pigment. Scents of pear, apple, and melon with some pepper and arugula tinges can be traced from these wines.

Pinot Noir

Pinot Noir has a reputation for is fickleness; while it produces some of the world's best wines—like the Burgundian red—it is also a challenging grape to grow and vinify. Here in California, it has taken many years to make truly extraordinary Pinot Noir, however, much progress has been made over the last decade or so. These wines tend to be less tannic and have less pigment than a Cabernet or Merlot, so the wines are rather light. Typically drinkable after two to five years, the finest Pinot Noir will improve some years after.

Port

Port wine is made in the Northern part of Portugal along the Douro river. These rare sweet red wines are made with dozens of Portuguese traditional grapes including Touriga Nacional, Touriga Franca, and Tinta Roriz. The grapes are collected and fermented together in open tanks where the grapes are stomped daily as the wine begins to ferment.

Riesling

Riesling is the classic white wine grape from Germany and known for its floral perfume. Depending on where they're made, they can be crisp and bone-dry, full-bodied and spicy or luscious and sweet. Well-made Rieslings can be aged for decades.

Rosés (Blush Wines)

Rosés, also called blush wines, are light pink wines made from several red wine grapes. They get their color from a very short period of contact with the grape skins during the wine-making process. Rosés are light and can be very dry or somewhat sweet. They are best served well-chilled.

Roussanne

Roussanne is a white wine grape grown originally in the Rhône wine region in France, where it is often blended with Marsanne. The berries are distinguished by their russet color when ripe—roux is French for the reddish-brown color russet, and is probably the root for the variety's name.

Sangiovese

Sangiovese is an Italian varietal; going from offbeat to complete sensation during the nineties, its traces of black tea, spice, and cherries enrich an assortment of dishes. Many wineries produce Sangioveses often ready to indulge oneself in upon release, making this varietal easy and adaptable to any occasion.

Sauvignon Blanc

Sauvignon Blanc grapes make wines that can emerge under two names: Sauvignon Blanc and Fumé Blanc. These wines are becoming progressively more popular because of their unique character that is often described as fruity and sweet, with well-balanced acidity. Similar to the Chardonnay grapes, one will find a scope of styles; some are crisp with more of an herbaceous flavor and others have a ripe pineapple-like lushness.

Sémillon

Semillon is a white grape originally from France, but currently grown worldwide. The grape is characterized by low acidity, thin skins and an almost oily texture. It is used in the production of both dry and sweet wines. Dry Sémillons are full-bodied, with combined flavors of citrus, honey and grass. For Sémillon to be able to produce sweet wine, the grapes need to have been affected by the Botyris fungus.

Sherry

Sherry comes from Andalusia, Spain. The wines are made using Palomino, Pedro Ximénez (a grape, not a person), and Moscatel grapes. Wines are produced using varying amounts of the three grapes and are purposefully oxidized so that they develop nutty aromatics.

Sparkling Wine

Sparkling Wine (carbonated and bubbly) can only be called "Champagne" if it is made in the region of France which is located just outside of Paris. To clarify, all Champagne is sparkling wine, but not all sparkling wine is Champagne.

Syrah

The Syrah, or Shiraz, grape is a dark-skinned grape grown in many regions across the globe. Whether labeled as Syrah or Shiraz, these strong flavored wines are quite popular. Though primarily used to make red wines, this variety harvests an assortment of flavors, depending on the diverse viticultural practices used to cultivate the grapes. These wines can produce succulent scents of chocolate and espresso, titillating aromas of violets and berries, and occasionally tones of black pepper.

Tempranillo

Tempranillo is red grape variety native of Spain. Tempranillo is currently grown worldwide and widely recognized as being capable of making palatable full-bodied reds. Tempranillo is the main grape variety used in Rioja. Tempranillo wines are ruby red in color, with aromas and flavors of dark berries, plum, tobacco, dried fig, cedar, leather and waxy herbs. Tempranillo is rarely drank on its own and is more often blended with Grenache.

Viognier

Viognier is a white grape variety currently grown worldwide, especially South Africa and New Zealand. It produces full-bodied wines with distinctive fruity and floral aromas and flavors of apricots, flowers, honeysuckle, ripe peaches and undernotes of musk. Viognier wines are low in acidity which makes them less amenable to ageing.

Zinfandel

Zinfandel is one of California's most versatile grape varieties. Much of the world's Zinfandel domain resides in Napa Valley. This varietal is vinified into light, easy-drinking red wines, some heavier, richly flavored versions that thrive with bottle aging, as well as white or "blush" wines, all with their own unique charm.

All About Blends

We are seeing something like a golden age of wine blends in California. It's a creative, exciting time because so many winemakers are exploring blends as they have never before.

Varietal blends offer winemakers an added level of artistic freedom that can be done during a blending process with wine from tanks and barrels, or can even be done in the field during harvest (a "field blend").

Why do red blends dominate the market? Where are the white blends? Reds may be the star because there are so many more choices of red wines for blending. Also, Chardonnay is the top wine in America, and winemakers tell us consumers do not want to see their Chardonnay muddled up with any other wine.

Most blends are related to certain regions (the Rhône Valley, Italy, Champagne). But California winemakers have begun to break those barriers. They're blending Zinfandel with Cabernet Sauvignon or Petite Sirah or Syrah, or all three. Tempranillo, a Spanish red, may be blended with Cabernet Sauvignon.

Please note that because of the wide range and unique variety of blended wines throughout California's wineries, our guidebooks do not list them in the A to Z wineries section. There are just too many to list! Nonetheless, be sure to ask or inquire about a winery's blends when tasting, searching, or buying so you don't miss out.

Here's the short list of red varietal blends you'll find with California wines today:

Bordeaux

Red varietals include Cabernet Sauvignon, Merlot, Cabernet Franc, Petit Verdot and Malbec. White Varietals include Sauvignon Blanc and Sémillon.

Côtes du Rhône

Red varietals include GSM: Grenache, Syrah, Mourvèdre and even Viognier (a white wine). White Varietals include Marsanne, Roussanne, and Viognier.

Super Tuscans

Red varietals include Sangiovese, Merlot, Syrah, or Cabernet Sauvignon.

Rosé (Blush) Wines

A rosé (or blush wine) is a type of wine that incorporates some of the color from the grape skins, but not enough to qualify it as a red wine. The pink color can range from a pale "onionskin" orange to a vivid near-purple, depending on the grape varieties used and winemaking techniques. Usually, the wine is labelled rosé in French, Portuguese, and English-speaking countries, rosado in Spanish, or rosato in Italian.

There are three major ways to produce rosé wine: skin contact, saignée, and blending. Rosé wines can be made still, semi-sparkling or sparkling and with a wide range of sweetness levels from highly dry Provençal rosé to sweet White Zinfandels and blushes. Rosé wines are made from a wide variety of grapes and can be found all around the globe.

When rosé wine is the primary product, it is produced with the skin contact method. Black-skinned grapes are crushed and the skins are allowed to remain in contact with the juice for a short period, typically two to twenty hours. The grape must is then pressed and the skins discarded, rather than left in contact throughout fermentation (as with red wine making). The longer the skins are left in contact with the juice, the more intense the color of the final wine.

Sparkling Wines

There are two main ways these carbonated/bubbly wines are produced: the traditional method and the Charmat method.

The traditional method is used when the still wine is first bottled, then additional yeast and sugar are added during a secondary fermentation. Once incorporated, the yeast ferments the sugar into alcohol until it is dry and generates CO_2, creating bubbles within the bottle.

The Charmat method was developed during the turn of the 20th century. It allows the second fermentation to take place in a pressurized tank, instead of the bottle.

It is important to know three of the most well-known sparkling wine regions: Prosecco and Cava. While these wines are all carbonated, there are key details that differentiate them.

Champagne

Champagne is a very specific varietal of sparkling wine. For sparkling to be classified as the wine must be produced in the Champagne region of northern France and meet the winemaking requirements of the region. Champagne has coined the term "méthode Champenoise" in regard to its production process. It goes through the same system as the traditional method.

Prosecco

Prosecco is an Italian-made sparkling wine and is produced using Prosecco or Glera grapes. By European Union law, the wine must be produced in northeast Italy, traditionally the Veneto region, to be called Prosecco. This wine typically uses the Charmat method in order to produce a youthful and clean wine.

Cava

Cava is a wonderful and flavorful sparkling wine from Spain. Cava is most comparable to Champagne in both taste and production, with the biggest difference being the grapes. Its naming restrictions require it to be made in the traditional method.

There are plenty of other sparkling wines that do not fall into one of these three categories. Some of the most popular sparkling regions are the United States, New Zealand, Australia and Germany.

Late Harvest / Desert Wines

Late harvest and dessert wines are made from grapes that are left on the vine even after they've reached their peak ripeness. When grapes are (quite literally) left hanging, they become sweeter over time as each individual grape dehydrates and the sugar content becomes more concentrated.

Late harvest grapes (typically picked 1-2 months after the regular harvest time) are used to make a wine that contains both higher residual sugar and higher potential alcohol than standard table wines. Technically, any wine grape can be harvested late (Chardonnay, Syrah, Pinot Gris, etc.), but you'll tend to see certain grapes chosen over others due to their ability to process exceptionally high-quality late harvest wines.

Here are four exceptional grape varieties used for late harvest wines that are well worth seeking out: Muscat, Riesling, Sauternais, and Vidal Blanc.

Wine Label Information

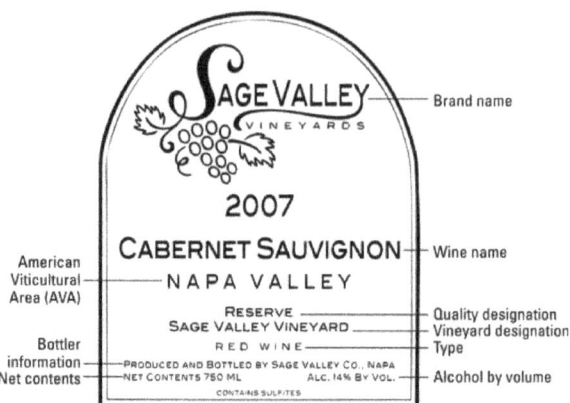

Wine labels from the United States are relatively straightforward and easy to understand, but there are strict laws governing what they must and must not show. The typical label shows the wine's producer, vintage, region of origin, and grape variety (e.g., Pinot Noir). Above is an example of an American wine label from a California winery, and below that an overview of US wine classifications and labeling laws.

American wine labeling laws are managed by the TTB (Alcohol and Tobacco Tax and Trade Bureau), the government bureau principally responsible for setting and monitoring alcohol-related taxes. By law, bottles of United States wine must be marked with a brand name, wine type, alcohol content, bottle volume, sulfite content, and the producer's name and address.

Essentials of Wine Making & Tasting

Wine making has been around for thousands of years. In its basic form, wine production is a natural process that requires very little human intervention. Mother Nature provides everything that is needed to make wine; it is up to humans to embellish, improve, or totally obliterate what nature has provided, to which anyone with extensive wine tasting experience can attest.

There are five basic stages or steps to making wine: harvesting, crushing and pressing, fermentation, clarification, and then aging and bottling.

Undoubtedly, one can find endless deviations and variations along the way. In fact, it is the variants and little deviations at any point in the process that make life interesting. They also make each wine unique and ultimately contribute to the greatness or ignominy of any particular wine.

The steps for making white wine and red wine are basically the same, with one exception. The making of rosé wines and fortified or sparkling wines is also another matter; both require additional human intervention to succeed.

The Harvest

Harvesting or picking is certainly the first step in the actual wine making process. Without fruit there would be no wine, and no fruit other than grapes can produce annually a reliable amount of sugar to yield sufficient alcohol to preserve the resulting beverage, nor have other fruits the requisite acids, esters and tannins to make natural, stable wine on a consistent basis.

For this reason and a host more, most winemakers acknowledge that wine is made in the vineyard, at least figuratively. The process of making fine wine requires that the grapes are harvested at a precise time, preferably when physiologically ripe. A combination of science and old-fashioned tasting usually go into determining when to harvest, with consultants, winemakers, vineyard managers, and proprietors all having their say.

Harvesting can be done mechanically or by hand. However, many estates prefer to hand harvest, as mechanical harvesters can often be too tough on the grapes and the vineyard. Once the grapes arrive at the winery, reputable winemakers will sort the grape bunches, culling out rotten or under-ripe fruit before crushing.

Crushing and Pressing

Crushing the whole clusters of fresh ripe grapes is traditionally the next step in the wine making process. Today, mechanical crushers perform the time-honored tradition of stomping or trodding the grapes into what is commonly referred to as must. For thousands of years, it was men and women who performed the harvest dance in barrels and presses that began grape juice's magical transformation from concentrated sunlight and water held together in clusters of fruit to the most healthful and mystical of all beverages—wine.

As with anything in life, change involves something lost and something gained. By using mechanical presses, much of the romance and ritual has departed this stage of wine making, but one need not lament too long due to the immense sanitary gain that mechanical pressing brings to wine making.

Mechanical pressing has also improved the quality and longevity of wine, while reducing the winemaker's need for preservatives. Having said all this, it is important to note that not all wine begins life in a crusher. Sometimes, winemakers choose to allow fermentation to begin inside uncrushed whole grape clusters, allowing the natural weight of the grapes and the onset of fermentation to burst the skins of the grapes before pressing the uncrushed clusters.

Up until crushing and pressing the steps for making white wine and red wine are essentially the same. However, if a winemaker is to make white wine, he or she will quickly press the must after crushing in order to separate the juice from the skins, seeds, and solids. By doing so unwanted color (which comes from the skin of the grape, not the juice) and tannins cannot leach into the white wine.

Essentially, white wine allows very little skin contact, while red wine is left in contact with its skins to garner color, flavor, and additional tannins during fermentation, which of course is the next step.

Fermentation

Fermentation is indeed the magic at play in the making of wine. If left to its own devices must or juice will begin fermenting naturally within 6-12 hours with the aid of wild yeasts in the air. In very clean, well-established wineries and vineyards this natural fermentation is a welcome phenomenon.

However, for a variety of reasons, many winemakers prefer to intervene at this stage by inoculating the natural must. This means they will kill the wild and sometimes unpredictable natural yeasts and then introduce a strain of yeast of personal choosing in order to predict the end result more readily.

Regardless of the chosen path, once fermentation begins, it normally continues until all of the sugar is converted to alcohol and a dry wine is produced. Fermentation can require anywhere from ten days to a month or more.

The resulting level of alcohol in a wine will vary from one locale to the next, due to the total sugar content of the must. An alcohol level of 10% in cool climates versus a high of 15% in warmer areas is considered normal. Sweet wine is produced when the fermentation process stops before all of the sugar has been converted into alcohol. This is usually a conscious, intentional decision on the part of the winemaker.

Clarification

Once fermentation is completed, the clarification process begins. Winemakers have the option of racking or siphoning their wines from one tank or barrel to the next in the hope of leaving the precipitates and solids called pomace in the bottom of the fermenting tank. Filtering and fining may also be done at this stage.

Filtration can be done with everything from a course filter that catches only large solids to a sterile filter pad that strips wine of all life. Fining occurs when substances are added to a wine to clarify them. Often, winemakers will add egg whites, clay, or other compounds to wine that will help precipitate dead yeast cells and other solids out of a wine. These substances adhere to the unwanted solids and force them to the bottom of the tank. The clarified wine is then racked into another vessel, where it is ready for bottling or further aging.

Aging and Bottling

The final stage of the wine making process involves the aging and bottling of wine. After clarification, the winemaker has the choice of bottling a wine immediately, which is the case for Beaujolais Nouveau, or he or she can give a wine additional aging as in the case of Grand Cru Bordeaux and great Napa Valley Cabernet Sauvignon.

Further aging can be done in the bottle, stainless steel or ceramic tanks, large wooden ovals, or small barrels, commonly called barriques. The choices and techniques employed in this final stage of the process are nearly endless, as are the end results. However, the common result in all cases is wine. Enjoy!

Do's and Don'ts of Tasting Wine

Hopefully our winery guide has directed you to where you need to be to start wine tasting. If you're a novice tasting wines at tasting room for the first time, we made it easy for you to find them. If you're a wine connoisseur with an extensive knowledge and appreciation of wine, the digital versions of this winery guide can help you filter the types of wine varietals you're looking for.

From novice, to expert, to everyone in between, at California Winery Guides we believe the only critic you should listen to is yourself.

For wine tasting at the South Coast's 240 plus wineries with tasting and urban tasting rooms (sometimes referred to as wine bars), expect to pay $25 per person and higher Monday-Friday and $30 per person and higher Saturday-Sunday that includes 5 to 6 tastings.

For wine tasting reservations, the Tock app is a platform for booking wine tasting and restaurant reservations. Tock also offers a companion app for businesses to manage reservations, guest lists, and other aspects of their operations. So once you've arrived for wine tasting, what comes next?

From commercials to the movie screen, everyone has seen the classic scene of a diner swirling their wine around the glass, then diving nose first into it to inhale the wine's secrets. For most, the order of these simple actions is irrelevant, but to a wine expert like Madeline Puckett at Wine Folly (for a deep dive into wines, check out her co-authored book along with fellow writer Justin Hammack titled *Wine Folly: The Essential Guide to Wine*), the following steps for tasting wine are as important as the actions themselves.

The Swirl

DO!

The first and most important step. Take the glass by the bottom of the stem and swirl! This will release the flavors and aromas of the wine.

The swirl also causes air to mix with the wine, which causes it to "open up" by allowing some of the alcohol vapors to dissipate. If you've ever used rubbing alcohol to sanitize a cut, you know how powerful a scent alcohol is.

By swirling, you cut down the impact of the alcohol smell and allow the more subtle aromas of the wine to shine.

DON'T!

Swirl the glass for longer than 5 to 6 seconds, it isn't needed. Remember it's a glass of wine, not a mixed drink.

While it can seem rudimentary (or even cliché), swirling is essential. To see for yourself, just take a sip of wine before swirling it. Then, cleanse your palate with some water, swirl the wine like a Frenchman, and take another sip. Take note of what's changed.

The difference in aromas and flavors is nearly impossible to miss! So don't forget to swirl! When serving, it might even be helpful to give this tip to your guest and quickly explain the benefits.

Not only will it increase their wine experience, but it will also make you appear very knowledgeable.

The Smell

DO!

Stick your nose in it! Not literally, but knowing what the wine smells like will help you pair the wine with food. Note the first things the wine reminds you of. Is it fruity, flowery, herbal, spicy, buttery?

DON'T!

Taste the wine before smelling it. The wine aroma is important to the experience of tasting, so get to the know the smell before the taste.

The Taste

First impressions matter. And once the wine has introduced itself to you with smell, then you can take your findings from the first steps and you are finally ready for the best part, tasting

DO!

Take a small sip of the wine, lightly swish it around your mouth, and swallow. This warms up the wine and enhances the wine's flavor profile.

While the wine is swishing in your mouth, breath steadily through your nose. This activates your sense of smell which is a big part of tasting and allows your taste buds to be more perceptive.

DON'T!

Gulp! The worst way to taste wine is by chugging it. Pace yourself. This method means you won't have the opportunity to enjoy the full experience of the complex flavors wine has to offer.

Drinking & Driving

To cut down on commute time, and help you practice wine tasting closer to home, we've included urban wineries close by which take much less time to get to than the traditional wineries spread out throughout the countryside. If you're new to wine tasting, the urban tasting room is a great place to start wine tasting, learn about wines first hand, and have fun doing it.

DO!

Moderation is key. Assign a designated driver.

DON'T!

Don't drink and drive.

Glossary of Wine Terminology

Do wines have arms and a face along with a body, nose and legs? Is terroir a type of dog breed? Wine lingo is expansive, and can feel very high-brow for describing fermented grapes. When a Sommelier or waiter / waitress comes to your table at a restaurant and begins rambling off fancy French words, wine can easily begin to feel intimidating and inaccessible.

Don't feel intimated! Use the list below to show how much you know—and see how far you go.

Acid–A key element of wine present in all grapes. When acid is balanced, wine is fresh and has a long life. Wines low in acidity taste flabby.

Age–The process of maturing in wines. As white wines age, they turn to a golden amber color. Reds usually begin with a purple tone, turning to a deep red brick red color depending on the grape.

Alcohol–Alcohol is the natural by-product of fermentation. It is one of the main components of taste along with acids, residual sugar and tannin.

American Viticultural Area (AVA)–When a AVA is designated on a wine label, 85% of the grapes used to make that wine must have come from that AVA. If a non-AVA Appellation or region is designated on a wine label, at least 75% of the grapes must come from that area.

Anthocyanin–One of the phenolics present in wine is the red and blue pigments found in the skins of dark grape varieties.

Appellation–The region where a specific grape is grown. Geography and climate combine to produce flavors and style characteristics, which are unique to a region.

Appellations–A geographically-based name for a winegrowing region that is believed to show unique characteristics of soil, climate and more. In the United States, appellation names such as Napa Valley are approved by the Bureau of Alcohol, Tobacco and Firearms. The term "sub-appellation" is used informally to refer to a smaller appellation wholly contained within a larger one and these are identified by AVAs.

Aroma–What gives a wine its distinctive "nose" or "bouquet."

Astringent–High tannic acid content giving a furry mouth puckering sensation.

Barrel–Equals 60 gallons of wine and each barrel contains 300 bottles, resulting in 25 cases.

Balance–All elements of a wine are in harmony, with no one element dominating. Acid is balanced against the sweetness, fruit is in balance with oak and tannin, and alcohol is balanced against both acidity and flavor.

Blending–The art of mixing different wines to create a better overall wine.

Blind Tasting–Wine tasting term for tasting wine from bottles with their labels hidden.

Blush wine–Light, slightly sweet or sometimes dry wine, either white or rosé, made from dark skinned grapes.

Body–The body of a wine refers to how big and bold and heavy it is.

Bottle-Aging–Maturing a wine in the bottle as opposed to a tank or barrel. Some wines may improve in the bottle for ten or more years.

Bouquet–The combination of aromas from wine generally including the more complex scents of bottle aged wine.

Breathe–When wine is poured from the bottle into another container, such as a wineglass or carafe, it mixes with air, releasing aromas which become more pronounced as time passes. Well made, young wines will improve and "open up" with an hour or more to breath.

Bud Break–The stage of the growing season, usually early spring in the Napa Valley, when tiny shoots emerge from their buds.

Buttery–The buttery taste of a white wine that has gone through malolactic fermentation, usually found in Chardonnay wine.

Case–12 (750 ml) bottles of wine.

Cedar–The term denoting the woody aromas found in red wines.

Chambrer–A term describing opening a bottle of wine so it can come into contact with the air and reach room temperature. From the French meaning "Allow to breathe."

Citrusy–An aroma and flavor of citrus fruits, often of grapefruit, generally found in white wines made from grapes grown in cooler regions of California.

Clarification–The process of clearing a wine that involves binding cloudy substances and particles, which then settle on the bottom, becoming sediment.

Clone–The offspring of grape vines that contains the genetic material of the parent. There are many clones with different characteristics for each grape variety.

Cloudy–Opposite of clear and considered a fault in wine.

Complexity–When a wine is rich, deep in flavors, nuanced and well balanced.

Corked–A cork may become contaminated with TCA and impart the taste of cork on the wine. Screw caps and synthetic corks have fewer TCA contamination problems.

Creamy–Refers to the silky taste of wines, usually white, that are subjected to malolactic fermentation as opposed to the tart or crisp flavors found in wines that are made without this process.

Crisp–A term used when wine has a pronounced but pleasing tartness or acidity. Generally used to describe white wine.

Crush–The season when the grapes are harvested and made into wine.

Cuvée–A term for the initial pressing of the grapes. Also a term for a blend of high-quality wines.

Decanting–Pouring wine slowly from the bottle into a carafe, which adds oxygen and separates the wine from the sediment.

Dry–A term meaning the lack of sweetness in a wine. However in Champagne it denotes a sweeter wine.

Enology—The science of wine production. Also spelled Oenology.

Fermentation—The process of winemaking that turns the sugar in the grapes into alcohol and carbon dioxide.

Fining—The process of clearing a wine that involves binding cloudy particles, which then settle and becoming sediment. Same as clarification.

Flat—A wine-tasting term denoting very low acid wine and lacking flavor.

Flavones—One of the phenolics found in wine are the yellow pigments in small amounts in all pale and dark skinned grape varieties.

Flinty—A stone or mineral like character used often to describe French Chablis and Sauvignon Blanc.

Floral—A wine-tasting term indicating the aroma or taste of flowers, mostly used to describe white wines.

Forward—Wine-tasting term indicating fruitiness in a wine and is ready to drink.

French Oak—The classic wood flavors of vanilla and cedar that come from wine stored in wood barrels. Different French forests impart slightly different characteristics to the wine.

Fresh—Describes the lively fruity acidity of a good young wine.

Full-bodied—A wine-tasting term denoting a wine that fills the mouth and palate.

Glycerin—A natural by-product of the fermentation process, giving wine a sweet taste on the tongue, and a smooth sensation in the mouth.

Grafting—The process of physically connecting two plants or pieces of plant tissue together to grow as one. In viticulture, grafting is often used to join a rootstock with a vine variety.

Grassy—The taste of fresh hay frequently found in Sauvignon Blanc.

GSM—Is a short-hand reference for a red wine blended from Grenache, Syrah, and Mourvèdre.

Herbaceous—The smell or taste of herbs found in Cabernet Sauvignon and Sauvignon Blanc.

Late Harvest—Wines made from grapes harvested later than normal with higher sugar levels.

Lees–The sediment remaining in the tank or barrel after fermentation.

Legs–Swirling a wineglass filled with wine will produce rivulets, arches or legs.

Library Wines–Are portions of vintages held back by wineries to be re-released years after their debut.

Maceration–Part of the fermentation process where grape skins, seeds and stems are steeped for hours or weeks before pressing. The process extracts color, tannin and aromas into the must.

Maderized–A wine that shows signs of oxidation, including a brown color and stinky nose.

Mash–The pulp of the grape, including skins and seeds, that settles in a fermentation tank or barrel.

Meritage–Combining the words "merit" and "heritage," a blend made from several varieties of quality grapes, usually the Bordeaux varietals- Cabernet Sauvignon, Merlot, Cabernet Franc, Petite Verdot and Malbec.

Méthode Champenoise–The time-consuming, secondary fermentation process that takes place inside the bottle to create sparkling wine. Developed in Champagne France.

Must–Raw, unfermented, grape juice.

Natural Wine–A generalized term for wine made with sustainably grown grapes and low intervention winemaking; meaning no sulfites or additives. So basically a wine that's produced by adding nothing, nor removing anything from it. A lot of big wine producers get away with adding chemicals and what not to wine to impact color or taste–Maker only works with independent, smaller producers, who do no such thing!

Noble Rot–Botrytis Cinerea. A fungus or mold that causes grapes to shrivel and the grape sugars and acids to become concentrated. Excellent honey flavored dessert wines are made from these grapes.

Non-Vintage–A blend of multiple harvests.

Nose–The overall scent of a wine.

Nouveau–A tradition in Beaujolais France where wines are fermented quickly, bottled and rushed to market for the Fall and Winter holidays.

Oenology–The science of wine production. Also spelled Enology.

Organic wine–Wines that are produced using organic farming principles or biodynamic practices are often generalized as organic wines. If they're accompanied with the word natural, it likely means they haven't been filtered, meaning they may appear a bit cloudier or have sediment towards the bottom of the bottle, and there are no additional additives.

Oxidation–The result of too much oxygen in the wine, causing color change and loss of freshness.

pH Value–A chemical measurement of the intensity of acidity in a wine. Low pH wines have more intense acids and are better candidates for aging.

Phenolics–Substances extracted from grape skins that provide the color and texture for red wine, specifically, anthocyanins, flavones and tannins.

Phylloxera–A small aphid that feeds on and fatally damages vine root systems.

Pierce's Disease–A fatal disease caused by a bacteria borne by the blue-green sharpshooter or glassy-winged sharpshooter, a leafhopper insect. The bacteria transmitted by the sharpshooter multiply and eventually block the vine's water-conducting systems.

Pressing–The process which separates the grape solids from the juice.

Punt–The name of the indentation found in the bottom of many wine bottles.

Racking–A natural and less disturbing clarification process that removes sediment by transferring the wine from one container to another until it is clear.

Residual Sugar–The natural sweetness of a wine, produced from the sugar not converted to alcohol during fermentation. Dry wines have little or no residual sugar while dessert wines can have 10% or more.

Rootstock–The root system to which a vine variety is grafted.

Rosé–Pink wine, usually fruity and made from black grapes with little skin contact, or from a blend of red and white wines.

Sediment–The accumulation of tannins and pigment deposits on a bottle of wine can be removed by decanting.

Solera–System for making brandies, sherry, port and other fortified wines that ensures the same quality year after year.

Sommelier–French term for a professional wine server.

Sparkling Wine—This bubbly wine is traditionally made from pinot noir, chardonnay and pinot munier. When made in the Champagne region of France, it's called Champagne.

Stabilization—A condition after fermentation where the wine has all the undesirable sediment removed and is clear in the bottle.

Sulfites—A derivative of sulfur and natural by-product of fermentation. Also used to clean and sterilize wine making equipment and to prevent wine from browning. Wines with over 10 ppm must state "contains sulfites" on the label.

Tannin—Provides the astringent mouth puckering effect in wines that is important in the aging of red wines. Tannin decreases as wine ages allowing the more subtle flavors of the wine to emerge.

Tartrates—The natural and harmless crystals that often form in barrels, bottles and on the cork. The safe glass like deposits are from tartaric acids present in the wine.

Taste—Four basic tastes detected by the tongue - sweet, salty, sour and bitter.

Terroir—This is a French term for the characteristics of the wine grape that result from all the environmental influences specific to where it was grown. The terroir is a connection between the final product and all the factors that influenced it.

Trellis System—The supporting framework on which a vine is trained to grow.

Urban Wineries—A recent phenomenon whereby a wine producer chooses to locate their winemaking facility in an urban setting within a city rather than in the traditional rural setting near the vineyards. With advances in technology and transportation, it is not a problem for an urban winery to grow their grapes in a remote location and then transport them to the urban facility for crushing, fermentation and aging.

Varietal—The grape variety used to make wine. In Europe, wines are usually named after the region in which the grapes are grown (i.e., Chianti, Burgundy). Elsewhere, wines are usually labeled with the name of the grape variety that the wine is made from (i.e., Cabernet, Chardonnay, etc.).

Vegetal—The smell or taste of green vegetables that can detract from a wines taste if too intense.

Veraison—When the red grapes turn color and white grapes become translucent. This is the phase of growth where the sugar begins to form.

Vinification–The production of wine from the harvest to the bottling.

Vintage Date–Refers to the year the grapes were harvested. Most wine regions require that at least 95% of the wine contain grapes harvested from that year.

Vintage–A term referring to the year in which the grapes were grown. Also can denote a wine from an exceptional year.

Vintner–A person who produces wine.

Viticulture–The science of growing grapes.

Wine-Tasting–How soil, climate, and weather affect different varieties of grapes, and how those factors are manifested in the taste of the wine. Wine-tasting breaks down into four basic steps of: 1) color and clarity of the wine, 2) smell which is referred to as aroma or the "nose," 3) taste, and 5) aftertaste.

Yeast–Micro-organisms responsible for fermentation converting sugar to alcohol and carbon dioxide. Yeasts naturally occur on grape skins though most winemakers used cultured yeasts for winemaking.

Yield–The amount of grapes produced from a particular vineyard.

Winery Maps & Resources

Winery Guide Maps

San Diego County: San Pasqual & Ramona Valley Wineries (West) Map

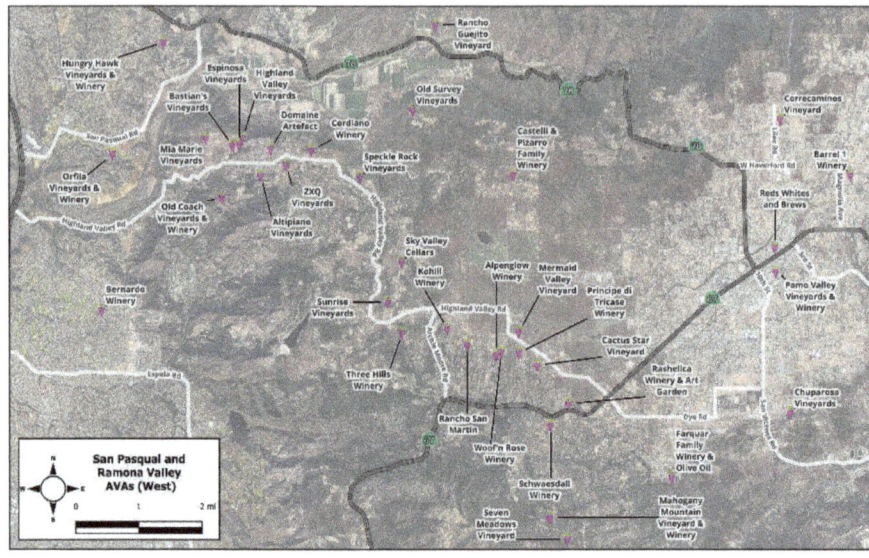

San Diego County: San Pasqual & Ramona Valley Wineries (East) Map

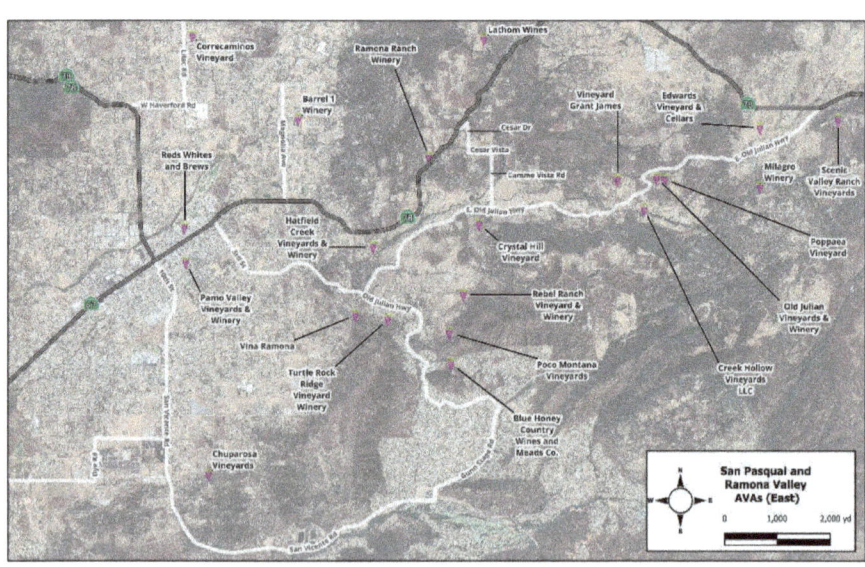

California South Coast Wineries Guide

San Diego County: Fallbrook-San Luis Rey Wineries Map

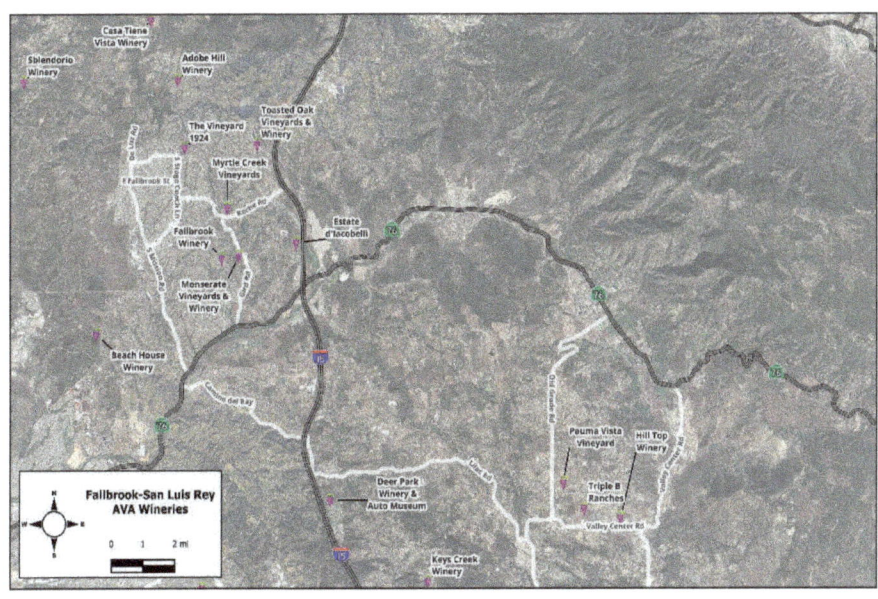

San Diego County: Escondido Wineries Map

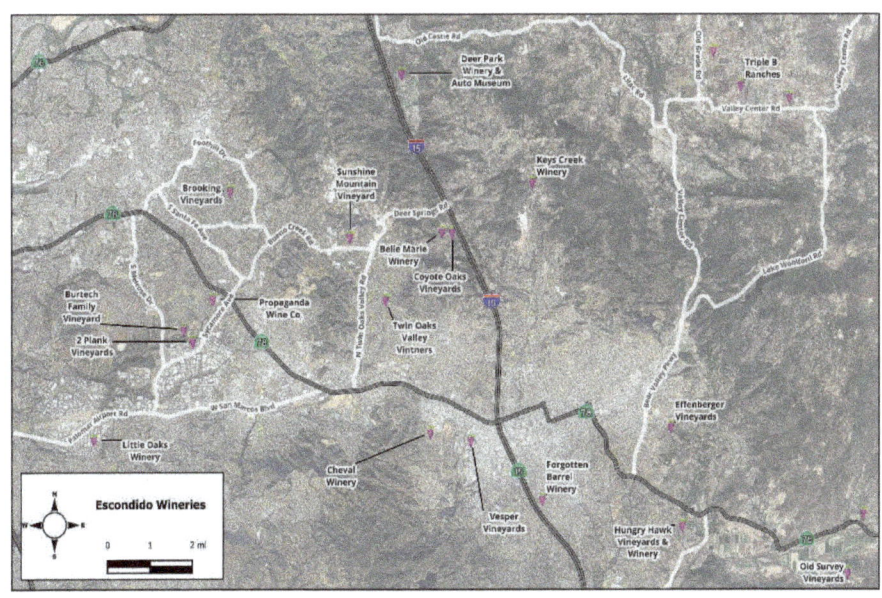

San Diego County: West Wineries Map

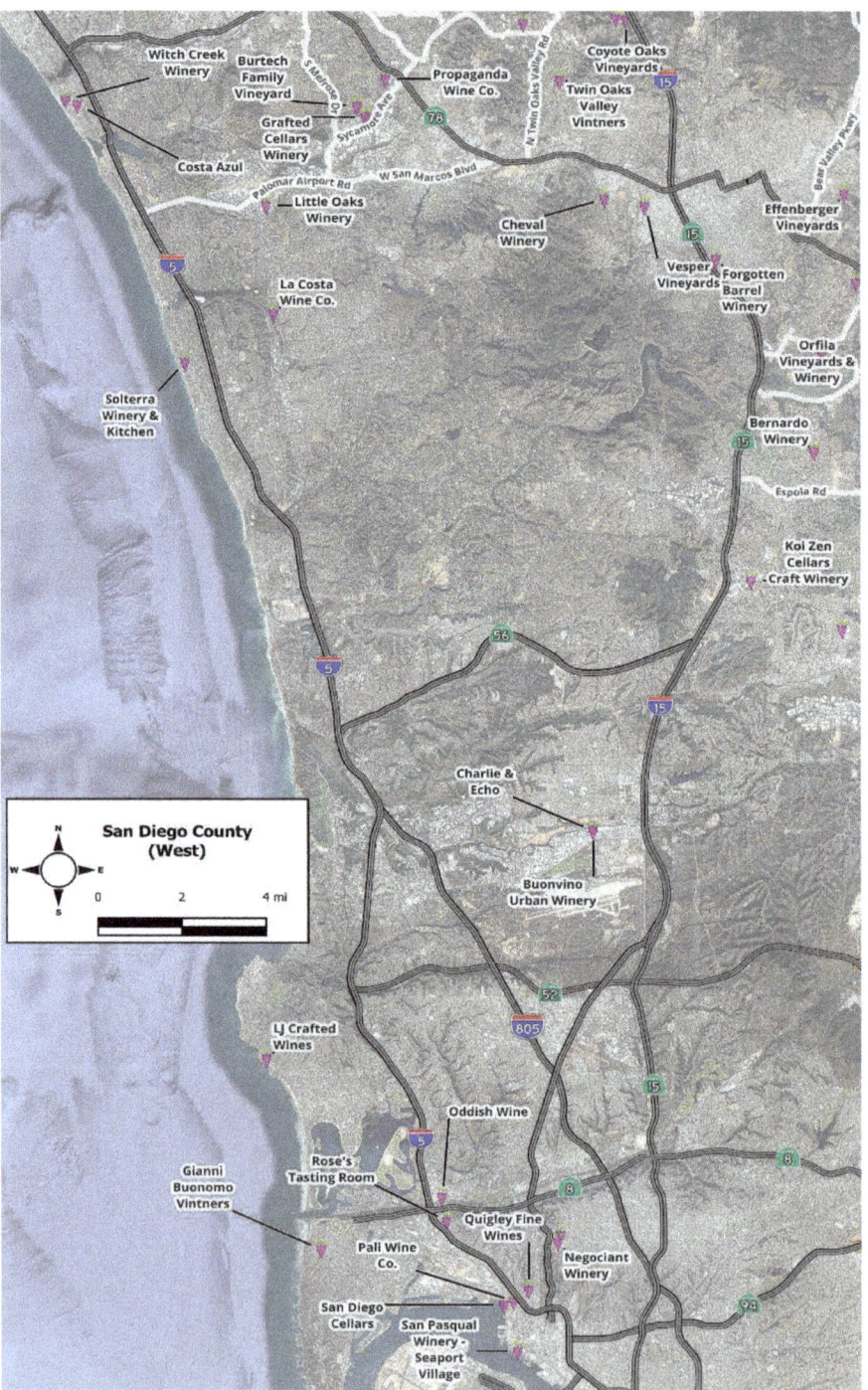

California South Coast Wineries Guide

San Diego County: Southeast Wineries Map

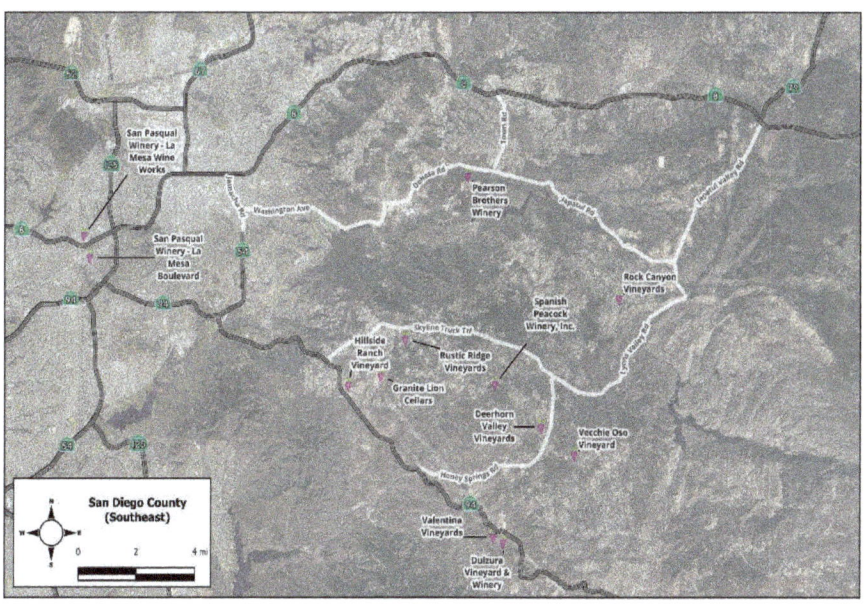

Riverside County: Temecula Wineries (West) Map

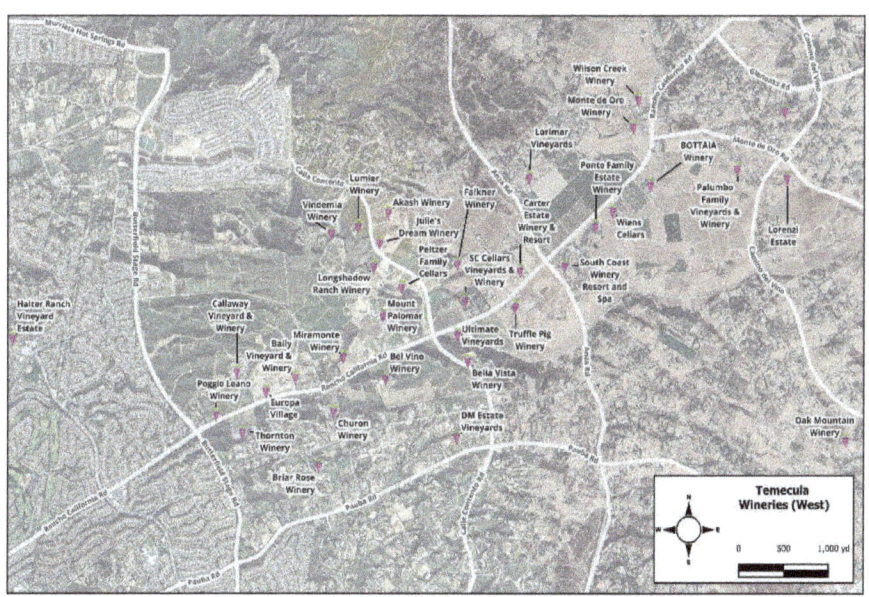

Riverside County: Temecula Wineries (East) Map

California South Coast Wineries Guide

Los Angeles County Wineries Map

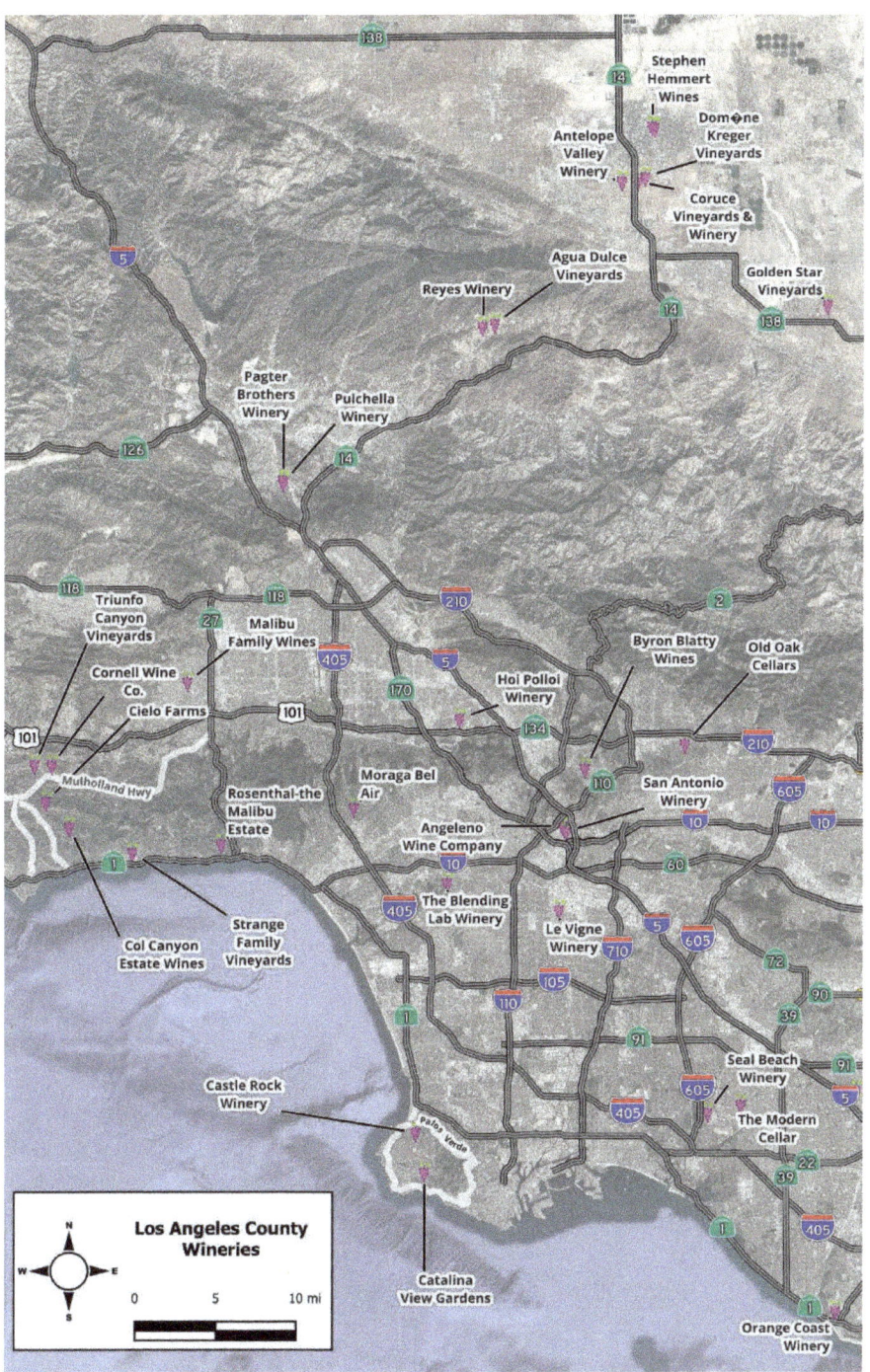

Los Angeles County Wineries

California South Coast Wineries Guide

Ventura County Wineries Map

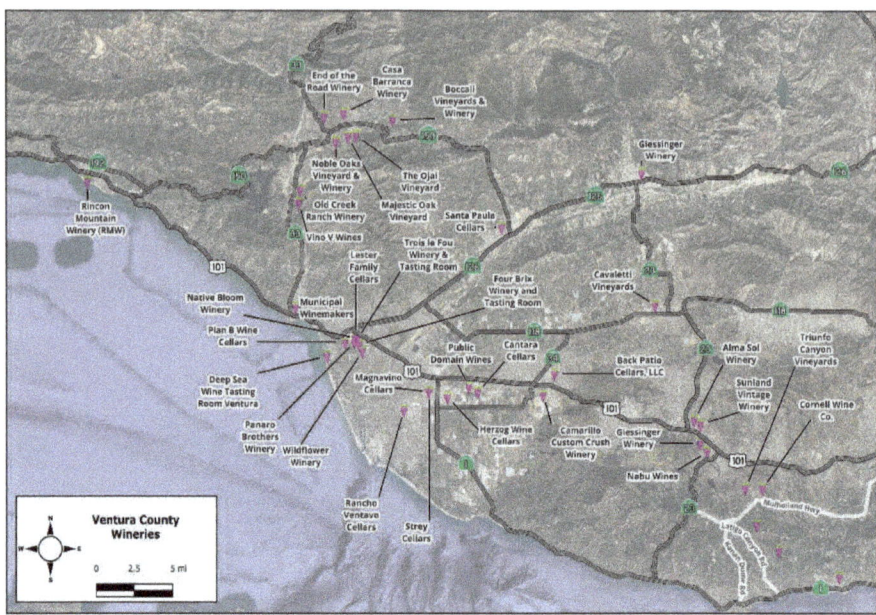

Orange County Wineries Map

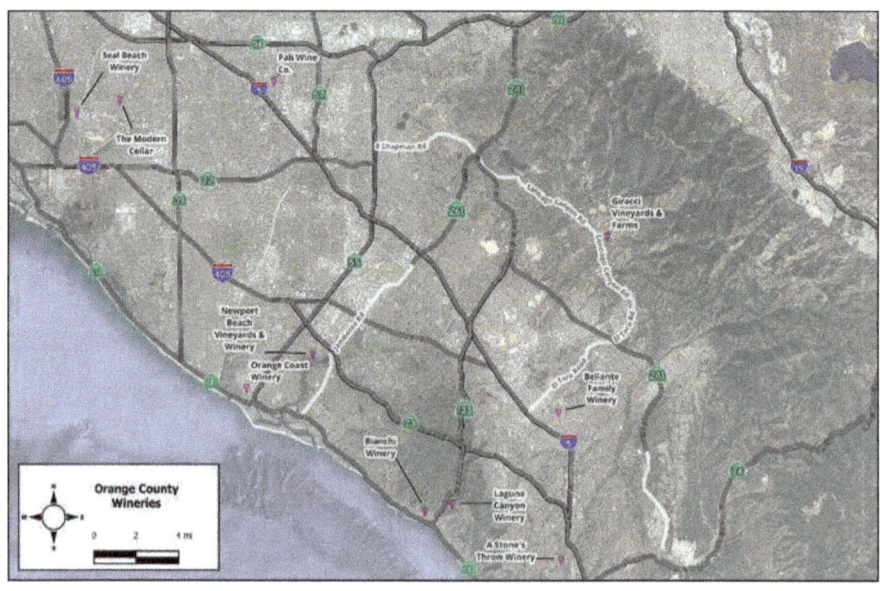

San Bernardino County Wineries Map

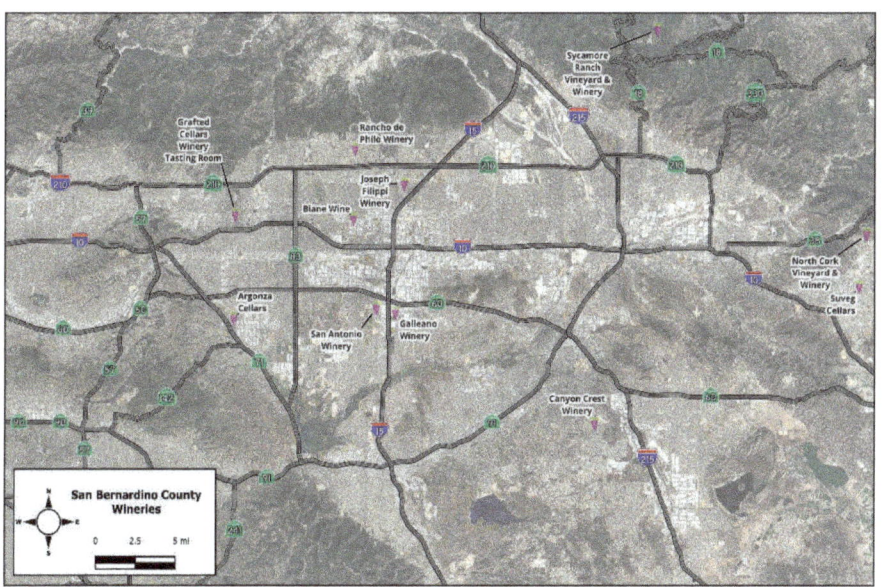

Winery Guide Resources

Alcoholic Beverage Control (ABC): https://www.abc.ca.gov/licensing/

Alcohol and Tobacco Tax and Trade Bureau (TTB): https://www.ttb.gov/

American Viticultural Areas of California: https://wineinstitute.org/wp-content/uploads/2023/07/CA-AVAs_FINAL-FOR-WEBSITE_7.13.2023.pdf

Antelope Valley Winegrowers Association (AVWA): https://www.avwinegrowers.org/Welcome.html

AVA Map Explorer: https://www.ttb.gov/ava

Basic Wine Terminology: https://www.getbackbar.com/basic-wine-knowledge

California Association of Winegrape Growers: https://www.cawg.org/Shared_Content/Resources/Regional_Associations.aspx

Early History of California Winemaking: https://www.totalwine.com/discover/learn/california-wine-regions

Grape Varieties, List of White and Red Wine: https://www.winetraveler.com/grape-varieties/

Los Angeles Vintners Association: https://www.lavintners.com/

Malibu Coast AVA: https://www.malibucoastava.com/

Ramona Valley Vineyard Association: https://ramonavalleyvineyards.com/

San Diego County Vintners Association: https://sandiegowineries.org/

State of the Wine Industry Report 2023: https://www.svb.com/trends-insights/reports/wine-report

Temecula Valley Winegrowers Association: https://www.temeculawines.org/

USA Wine Label Information: https://www.wine-searcher.com/wine-label-usa

Ventura County Winery Association: https://www.localwineevents.com/wine-food-and-drink-blogs/ventura-county-winery-association/1899

Wine Movies: https://www.sonoma.com/blog/best-wine-movies/

Wine Tasting Scorecards: https://www.wsetglobal.com/knowledge-centre/tasting-notes-app/

Women Winemakers of California: https://webpages.scu.edu/womenwinemakers/wineriesaz.php

Index of Wineries & Organizations

R

Ramona Ranch Winery · 55
Ramona Valley AVA · 24, 25
Rancho de Philo Winery · 125
Rancho Guejito Vineyard · 56
Rancho San Martin · 56
Rancho Ventavo Cellars · 103
Rashelica Winery & Art Garden · 56, 57
Raul Ramírez Bodegas Y Viñedos · 89
Record Family Wines · 57
Reds Whites and Brews · 57
Reyes Winery · 114
Rincon Mountain Winery · 103
Riverside County · 23, 70, 71, 72, 122, 155,
    159, 160
Riverside County: Temecula Wineries (East)
    Map · 155, 160
Riverside County: Temecula Wineries
    (West) Map · 155, 159
Robert Renzoni Vineyards · 89
Rock Canyon Vineyards · 57
Rosenthal – The Malibu Estate · 115
Rose's Tasting Room · 58
Rustic Ridge Vineyards · 58

S

Saddle Rock Malibu AVA · 106
San Antonio Winery · 115, 126
San Bernardino County · 23, 122, 124, 155,
    163
San Bernardino County Wineries · 124, 155,
    163
San Bernardino County Wineries Map · 155
San Diego County · 21, 23, 24, 25, 27, 29,
    32, 38, 42, 46, 48, 49, 51, 61, 67, 155,
    156, 157, 158, 159, 164
San Diego County AVA · 24, 25
San Diego County: Escondido Map · 155,
    157
San Diego County: Fallbrook-San Luis Rey
    AVA Map · 155
San Diego County: San Pasqual and Ramona
    Valley AVAs (East) Map · 155, 156
San Diego County: San Pasqual and Ramona
    Valley AVAs (West) Map · 155, 156
San Diego County: Southeast Map · 155,
    159

San Diego County: West Map · 155, 158
San Luis Rey AVA · 27, 28, 155, 157
San Pasqual Valley AVA · 24, 26
San Pasqual Winery – La Mesa Boulevard ·
    58
San Pasqual Winery – La Mesa Wine Works ·
    59
San Pasqual Winery – Seaport Village · 59
Santa Paula Cellars · 104
Sblendorio Winery · 60
Scenic Valley Ranch Vineyards · 60
Schwaesdall Winery · 60
Seal Beach Winery · 121
Shadow Mountain Vineyards · 61
Sierra Pelona Valley AVA · 106
Sierra Roble Winery & Vineyard · 61
Sky Valley Cellars · 61
Solterra Winery & Kitchen · 61
Somerset Vineyards & Winery · 89
South Coast AVA · 24, 25, 26
South Coast Winery Region AVAs · 21
South Coast Winery Region AVAs Map · 155
South Coast Winery Resort & Spa · 90
Spanish Peacock Winery, Inc. · 62
Speckle Rock Vineyards · 62
Stephen Hemmert Wines · 115, 116
Strange Family Vineyards · 116
Strey Cellars · 104
Sunland Vintage Winery · 104
Sunrise Vineyards · 63
Sunshine Mountain Vineyard · 63
Suveg Cellars · 126
Sycamore Ranch Vineyard & Winery · 127

T

Temecula Valley AVA · 27, 70
The Judgment of Paris · 14
Thornton Winery · 90
Three Hills Winery · 63
Toasted Oak Vineyards & Winery · 64
Trevi Hills Winery · 64
Triple B Ranches · 64, 65
Trois le Fou Winery & Tasting Room · 105
Truffle Pig Winery · 91
Turtle Rock Ridge Vineyard Winery · 65

www.ingramcontent.com/pod-product-compliance
Lightning Source LLC
Chambersburg PA
CBHW051521120626
46551CB00012B/1028